GREAT TASTES

SEAFOOD

First published in 2009 by Bay Books, an imprint of Murdoch Books Pty Limited
This edition published in 2010.

Murdoch Books Australia
Pier 8/9
23 Hickson Road
Millers Point NSW 2000
Phone: +61 (0) 2 8220 2000
Fax: +61 (0) 2 8220 2558
www.murdochbooks.com.au

Murdoch Books UK Limited
Erico House, 6th Floor
93–99 Upper Richmond Road
Putney, London SW15 2TG
Phone: +44 (0) 20 8785 5995
Fax: +44 (0) 20 8785 5985
www.murdochbooks.co.uk

Chief Executive: Juliet Rogers
Publishing Director: Kay Scarlett
Publisher: Lynn Lewis
Senior Designer: Heather Menzies
Designer: Wendy Inkster
Production: Kita George

ISBN: 9780681657793

PRINTED IN CHINA

IMPORTANT: Those who might be at risk from the effects of salmonella poisoning (the elderly, pregnant women, young children and those suffering from immune deficiency diseases) should consult their doctor with any concerns about eating raw eggs.

OVEN GUIDE: You may find cooking times vary depending on the oven you are using. For fan-forced ovens, as a general rule, set the oven temperature to 20°C (35°F) lower than indicated in the recipe.

GREAT TASTES

SEAFOOD

More than 120 easy recipes for every day

bay books

CONTENTS

STARTERS

CREAMY BACCALA AND GARLIC SPREAD

MAKES 500 ML (17 FL OZ/2 CUPS)

400 g (14 oz) salt cod (baccala)
 (see Note)

125 ml (4 fl oz/½ cup) olive oil

2 garlic cloves, roughly chopped

150 ml (5 fl oz) pouring cream

juice of ½ lemon

½ teaspoon thyme

freshly ground white pepper, to taste

1 Put the salt cod in a large, shallow dish and cover with plenty of cold water. Cover with plastic wrap and refrigerate for 2 days, changing the water twice a day.

2 Drain the salt cod and rinse again. Put in a large saucepan, cover with cold water and slowly heat over medium–low heat until nearly boiling. Cook, with just a few bubbles appearing, for 10 minutes. Try to prevent the water from boiling as this will toughen the cod. Drain and rinse under cold water until cold enough to handle. Remove the skin and bones, being careful to leave no bones in the flesh.

3 Meanwhile, heat the oil and garlic in a small saucepan over low heat for 3–4 minutes, or until the garlic becomes aromatic. Remove from the heat.

4 Put the salt cod in a small processor fitted with the metal blade and add the garlic. Whizz for 25–30 seconds, or until smooth. With the motor running, slowly add the oil. Add the cream and whizz in 5-second bursts until combined. Add the lemon juice, thyme and freshly ground white pepper, to taste, and whizz for 2–3 seconds, or until just combined.

5 Serve the spread with melba toast or crispbread and garnish with thyme sprigs. Store, covered, in the refrigerator for up to 3 days. Stir in a little warm cream to serve.

Note: Where possible, select fleshy pieces of salt cod rather than whole salted and dry cod — it's easier to handle and there's less wastage.

SALT AND PEPPER SQUID

SERVES 4

450 g (1 lb) whole squid or 250 g (9 oz) squid tubes

vegetable oil, for deep-frying

10 g (¼ oz) dried rice vermicelli

2 large red Asian shallots, sliced

potato flour or cornflour (cornstarch), for coating

2 small red chillies, sliced

SPICE MIX

1 teaspoon whole black peppercorns

1 teaspoon Sichuan peppercorns

2 teaspoons sea salt flakes

large pinch of Chinese five-spice

1   To prepare the squid, remove the intestines by firmly pulling on the tentacles. Pull out the clear quill, and remove the purple membrane by pulling on the flaps. Wash under running water to remove any ink and grit. Cut the tube in half lengthways. Lightly score the flesh in a criss-cross pattern, being careful not to cut all the way through, and then cut the squid roughly into 6 x 4 cm (2½ x 1½ inch) pieces. Refrigerate until ready to use.

2   To make the spice mix, grind the black and Sichuan peppercorns in a mortar and pestle or small food processor until the peppercorns are crushed. Add the sea salt and five-spice powder and mix well.

3   Fill a wok about one-third full of vegetable oil and heat to 180°C (350°F), or until a cube of bread dropped in the oil browns in 15 seconds. Break the dried vermicelli noodles up roughly and drop them into the hot oil — they will sizzle and float to the surface almost immediately. Remove from the oil, and drain on crumpled paper towels. Cook shallots in the wok until golden. Drain well; they will crisp on sitting.

4   Coat the squid in potato flour and drop into the hot oil. Cook for 30–60 seconds, or until lightly golden and crisp. Drain on crumpled paper towels. Coat the squid with 1–2 teaspoons of the spice mix, or to taste.

5   To serve, arrange the squid on a bed of crispy noodles, and top with the fried shallots and chilli slices. The extra spice mix can be served alongside, or can be stored in a jar for use another time.

FRAGRANT FISH IN BETEL LEAVES

MAKES 24

1 stem lemongrass, white part only, bruised

2 kaffir lime leaves, torn

500 ml (17 fl oz/2 cups) chicken stock

400 g (14 oz) blue eye cod fillet

90 g (3¼ oz/1½ cups) shaved fresh coconut meat

1 small handful Vietnamese mint

2 tablespoons chopped mint

3 red Asian shallots, finely chopped

24 betel leaves, washed and dried (see Note)

180 g (6½ oz) seaweed salad, to garnish (see Note)

DRESSING

1 tablespoon coconut vinegar or white wine vinegar

1 tablespoon lime juice

3 teaspoons fish sauce

2 teaspoons caster (superfine) sugar

1 small red chilli, seeded and finely chopped

1   **Put the lemongrass,** lime leaves and stock in a wok over medium–high heat and bring to a simmer. Add the fish and poach gently, turning once, for 10–12 minutes, or until the fish is just cooked through and flakes easily with a fork. Remove and set aside to cool, discarding the broth.

2   **To make the dressing,** combine the ingredients in a small bowl.

3   **In a large non-metallic bowl,** combine the coconut, mints and shallots. Gently flake the cooled fish into small pieces with a fork and add to the bowl. Pour on the dressing and stir gently until thoroughly combined.

4   **To serve,** put tablespoons of the fish salad on the betel leaves, garnish with seaweed salad. To eat, roll up the leaves to enclose the filling.

SESAME-COATED TUNA WITH WASABI MAYONNAISE

SERVES 4

WASABI MAYONNAISE

125 g (4½ oz/½ cup) Japanese
   mayonnaise

3 teaspoons wasabi paste

1 tablespoon Japanese soy sauce

2 teaspoons rice wine vinegar

500 g (1 lb 2 oz) fresh tuna, cut into
   2 cm (¾ inch) cubes

50 g (1¾ oz/⅓ cup) white sesame seeds

50 g (1¾ oz/⅓ cup) black sesame seeds

oil, for deep-frying

1 To make the wasabi mayonnaise, combine all the ingredients in a small bowl. Set aside until ready to serve.

2 Put the tuna in a bowl with the sesame seeds and toss to coat evenly.

3 Fill a wok one-third full of oil and heat to 180°C (350°F), or until a cube of bread dropped in the oil browns in 15 seconds. Deep-fry the cubes of tuna in three batches for 1–2 minutes, or until the tuna is lightly golden and still pink in the centre. Drain on crumpled paper towels. Serve with the wasabi mayonnaise.

Note: Serve the tuna on a platter with toothpicks for finger food or, if you prefer it as a starter, arrange the tuna on a bed of mixed salad leaves and drizzle with the mayonnaise.

FRIED WHITEBAIT

SERVES 4

500 g (1 lb 2 oz) whitebait

2 teaspoons sea salt

2 tablespoons plain
(all-purpose) flour

1½ tablespoons cornflour (cornstarch)

2 teaspoons finely chopped flat-leaf
(Italian) parsley

vegetable oil, for deep-frying

lemon wedges, for serving

1 **Combine the whitebait** and sea salt in a bowl and mix well. Cover and refrigerate until needed.

2 **Combine the sifted flours** and parsley in a bowl and season well with freshly ground black pepper.

3 **Fill a deep-fat fryer** or large saucepan one-third full of oil and heat to 180°C (350°F), or until a cube of white bread dropped into the oil browns in 15 seconds.

4 **Toss a third of the whitebait** in the flour mixture, shake off the excess flour, and deep-fry for 1½ minutes, or until pale and crisp. Drain well on crumpled paper towels. Repeat with the remaining whitebait.

5 **Just before serving**, reheat the oil to 190°C (375°C), or until a cube of white bread browns in 10 seconds, and fry the whitebait a second time, in batches, for 1 minute each batch, or until lightly browned. Drain on crumpled paper towels, salt lightly (this will help absorb any excess oil) and serve while hot with some lemon wedges.

SEAFOOD STUFFED SHIITAKE MUSHROOMS

SERVES 4–6

STUFFING

300 g (10½ oz) raw prawns (shrimp), peeled, deveined and finely chopped

150 g (5½ oz) minced (ground) chicken

50 g (1¾ oz) pork rind, very finely chopped (ask your butcher for this)

30 g (1 oz) ham, finely chopped

1 spring onion (scallion), finely chopped

2 large garlic cloves, crushed

1½ tablespoons finely chopped water chestnuts

1½ tablespoons finely chopped bamboo shoots

1½ teaspoons grated fresh ginger

1 tablespoon Chinese rice wine

1 tablespoon oyster sauce

1 tablespoon light soy sauce

2–3 drops of sesame oil

1 egg white, beaten until frothy

¼ teaspoon sugar

pinch of Chinese five-spice

white pepper, to taste

300 g (10½ oz) shiitake mushrooms (see Note)

1 litre (35 fl oz/4 cups) chicken stock

1 star anise

oyster sauce, to serve

toasted sesame seeds, to garnish (optional)

1 **To make the stuffing,** put the prawns, chicken, pork rind, ham, spring onion, garlic, water chestnuts, bamboo shoots, ginger, rice wine, oyster sauce, soy sauce, sesame oil, egg white, sugar, five-spice and white pepper in a bowl and combine well.

2 **Remove the stalks** from the shiitake and reserve. Generously fill each mushroom cap with stuffing, rounding the tops slightly. The amount of stuffing you use for each mushroom will differ depending on their size — if the mushrooms are very small you may have some mixture left over.

3 **Pour the chicken stock** and 500 ml (17 fl oz/2 cups) of water into a wok and add the star anise and reserved mushroom stalks. Bring to the boil over high heat, then reduce the heat and keep at a slow boil.

4 **Line a large steamer** with baking paper and punch with holes. Place the mushrooms in a single layer on top, filling side up. Cover with a lid, sit the steamer over the boiling stock mixture and steam for 15 minutes, or until the filling and the mushrooms are cooked through.

5 **Place on a serving platter** and pour on a little of the stock. Drizzle with a little oyster sauce and garnish with the sesame seeds.

Note: When purchasing fresh shiitake, choose mushrooms that are plump, with firm caps that curl under. Avoid those with shrivelled, dehydrated caps as they're past their peak. Choose mushrooms of a similar size so they cook evenly.

GRAVLAX

SERVES 12

55 g (2 oz/¼ cup) sugar

2 tablespoons coarse sea salt

1 teaspoon crushed black peppercorns

2.5 kg (5 lb 8 oz) good-quality salmon, filleted, skin on

1 tablespoon vodka or brandy

2 tablespoons very finely chopped dill

2 tablespoons chopped dill, extra

MUSTARD SAUCE

125 ml (4 fl oz/½ cup) olive oil

2 tablespoons Dijon mustard

1½ tablespoons cider vinegar

2 teaspoons chopped dill

1 teaspoon caster (superfine) sugar

1 **Combine the sugar,** salt and peppercorns in a small dish.

2 **Remove any pinbones** from the salmon with tweezers or your fingers. Pat dry with paper towels and lay a fillet skin-side down in a shallow tray.

3 **Sprinkle the fish** with half the vodka, rub half the sugar mixture into the flesh, then sprinkle with 2 tablespoons of the dill. Sprinkle the flesh side of the other salmon fillet with the remaining vodka and then rub the remaining sugar mixture into the flesh. Lay it flesh-side down on top of the other fillet. Cover with plastic wrap, place a heavy board on top and weigh the board down with three heavy tins so that the salmon is being flattened. Refrigerate for 24 hours, carefully turning it over after 12 hours.

4 **For the mustard sauce,** whisk all the ingredients together.

5 **Uncover the salmon** and lay both fillets on a board. Brush off all the dill and seasoning using a stiff pastry brush. Sprinkle with the extra dill and press it onto the flesh, shaking off any excess.

6 **Serve** whole or thinly sliced on an angle towards the tail, with the mustard sauce.

DEEP-FRIED SQUID WITH GINGER AND SHALLOTS

SERVES 4

500 g (1 lb 2 oz) cleaned squid tubes

1 teaspoon Chinese five-spice

2 teaspoons salt

1½ teaspoons sugar

3 garlic cloves, crushed

3 tablespoons lime juice

3 tablespoons light soy sauce

3 teaspoons sesame oil

peanut or vegetable oil, for deep-frying

20 g (¾ oz) fresh ginger, cut into julienne strips

2 red Asian shallots, finely sliced

1–2 red chillies, chopped

1 lime, quartered

1 Cut the squid down one side to open it out, and dry with paper towels. Using a sharp knife, score into a tight diamond pattern. Combine the five-spice powder, salt, sugar, garlic, lime juice, light soy sauce and sesame oil in a small saucepan, but don't heat it yet. Brush some of the mixture over the scored side of the squid. Leave to marinate for 45 minutes. Place squid scored-side-up on a flat surface and cut into bite-sized strips.

2 Fill a wok one-third full of oil and heat to 180°C (350°F), or until a cube of bread dropped in the oil browns in 15 seconds. Add the squid in batches and deep-fry for 50–60 seconds, or until golden brown. Drain on crumpled paper towels, then transfer to a serving bowl.

3 Add the ginger, shallots and chilli to the mixture in the saucepan and stir over medium heat for 1–2 minutes, or until fragrant. Spoon over the squid and serve at once with the lime wedges. Squeeze the juice over the squid just before eating.

SMOKED SALMON BRANDADE WITH TURKISH TOAST

SERVES 4–6

pide (Turkish/flat bread), to serve
olive oil spray

BRANDADE

2 small (200 g/7 oz) potatoes, cut into
   5 cm (2 inch) pieces

2 tablespoons olive oil

½ small red onion, chopped

2 garlic cloves, chopped

1 tablespoon capers, rinsed and
   squeezed dry

125 g (4½ oz) smoked salmon, roughly
   chopped

2 tablespoons chopped dill

2 tablespoons pouring cream

1 teaspoon grated lemon zest

1 tablespoon lemon juice

1 **Preheat the oven** to 180°C (350°F/Gas 4). Cut the bread into serving-sized pieces and split each horizontally. Lightly spray the cut sides with oil and arrange on a large baking tray. Toast for 12–15 minutes, or until crisp and golden.

2 **To make the brandade,** cook the potato cubes in a saucepan of boiling water for 8–10 minutes, or until tender. Drain and roughly chop with a flat-bladed knife.

3 **Heat the oil** in a small saucepan over low heat. Add the onion, garlic and capers and fry for 2–3 minutes. Transfer to a small processor fitted with the metal blade and add the warm potato and the salmon. Whizz in 2-second bursts for 15–20 seconds, or until roughly combined. Add the dill, cream, lemon zest and lemon juice. Season well with salt and freshly ground black pepper. Whizz for 10 seconds, or until the mixture is combined but still has some texture. Serve the brandade spread on the toast.

Note: Store the brandade, covered, in the refrigerator for up to 4 days. Bring to room temperature before serving.

OTAK-OTAK

MAKES 14

2 small dried red chillies

14 banana leaf portions, each
   16 x 12 cm (6¼ x 4½ inches)

450 g (1 lb) skinless fish fillets (use a firm
   white fish such as snapper)

1 stem lemongrass, cut into thirds

1 small onion, peeled and halved

1 large garlic clove, peeled

generous pinch of ground turmeric

1 teaspoon palm sugar or soft brown
   sugar

1 teaspoon ground coriander

1 teaspoon shrimp paste

1 tablespoon peanuts or unsalted
   macadamia nuts

1 tablespoon chopped mint

1 tablespoon chopped coriander
   (cilantro) leaves

3 tablespoons coconut milk

1 **Put 14 toothpicks in a bowl**, cover with cold water and leave to soak. Put the dried chillies in a small bowl, cover with boiling water and leave to soak.

2 **If the banana leaves** have been frozen they will be soft when thawed, but if they are fresh and tough, blanch them in boiling water for a minute to soften, then drain and refresh in cold water.

3 **Roughly chop the fish** and put in a food processor. Blend to a thick purée, then transfer to a mixing bowl. Drain the chillies and remove any stalks. Put the chillies in the processor with a generous pinch of salt and all the remaining ingredients except the banana leaves. Blend to a paste, then gently mix through the puréed fish.

4 **Heat the grill** (broiler) to medium, and drain the cocktail sticks. Put 2 tablespoons of the fish mixture in the middle of each banana leaf. Enclose the filling by folding the shorter sides into the middle so that they overlap. Tuck the two protruding ends underneath to make a small parcel. Secure the two ends with a cocktail stick.

5 **Put the parcels** on a baking tray, smooth-side-up, and grill for 5 minutes, or until the parcels are hot in the middle. Serve hot, or as a chilled snack.

Note: Make sure your banana leaves are well folded and tucked in or they may unfold as they cook, but try not to fold them too tightly as the filling needs a little room to expand. If you can't obtain banana leaves, use foil instead.

FISH TIKKA

SERVES 4

MARINADE
250 g (9 oz/1 cup) thick plain yoghurt

2 spring onions (scallions), finely chopped

1 tablespoon grated fresh ginger

2 garlic cloves, crushed

2 tablespoons lemon juice

1 teaspoon ground coriander

1 tablespoon garam masala

1 teaspoon paprika

1 teaspoon chilli powder

2 tablespoons tomato paste (concentrated purée)

1 teaspoon salt

500 g (1 lb 2 oz) skinless firm white fish fillets (such as sea bream, snapper or orange roughy)

2 onions, each cut into 8 chunks

2 small green or red capsicums (peppers), each cut into 8 chunks

lemon wedges, to serve

YOGHURT DRESSING
50 g (1¾ oz/about ⅓ cup) peeled, diced cucumber

1 tablespoon chopped coriander (cilantro) leaves

250 g (9 oz/1 cup) thick plain yoghurt

1 Combine all the marinade ingredients in a shallow non-metallic dish long enough and deep enough to hold eight long metal skewers.

2 Cut the fish into 24 bite-sized chunks. On each skewer, thread 3 fish pieces, 2 onion pieces and 2 capsicum pieces, alternating them as you go. Turn the skewers about in the marinade so that all the fish and vegetables are well coated. Cover and marinate in the refrigerator for at least 1 hour, or overnight if convenient.

3 Mix the yoghurt dressing ingredients together in a small bowl and set aside.

4 Heat the grill (broiler) to its highest setting. When the grill is very hot, lift the skewers out of the marinade and grill for 5–6 minutes, or until the fish is firm and slightly charred.

5 Serve with the yoghurt dressing and lemon wedges.

Note: The grill needs to be very hot when cooking this dish to impart an authentic smoky, slightly charred tandoor-like flavour.

ALGERIAN SARDINE PATTIES

MAKES 6

450 g (1 lb) fresh sardines, gutted

1 slice white bread

1 large garlic clove, crushed

2 tablespoons chopped parsley

pinch of cumin seeds

pinch of paprika

2 large eggs, lightly beaten

4 tablespoons plain (all-purpose) flour, plus extra, for dusting

oil, for brushing

lemon wedges, to serve

1   Using a sharp knife, slice each sardine up along the middle into two neat fillets, and scrape the flesh away from the skins. Using tweezers, remove as many bones as possible, then roughly chop the sardines and place in a bowl.

2   Put the bread in a food processor and blend into fine breadcrumbs, or chop finely by hand. Add to the fish with the garlic, parsley, cumin, paprika, egg, flour and a little salt, and mix together well. With lightly floured hands, form the mixture into six balls and sit them on a plate. Cover and refrigerate for 30 minutes.

3   Preheat a barbecue grill plate or flat plate to medium. Brush the hotplate with a little oil, then add the fish balls and flatten them out slightly into a pattie shape. Cook for 4–5 minutes on each side, or until golden brown and cooked through. Serve at once with the lemon wedges.

Note: You could also make these patties from herrings or mackerel.

VODKA AND JUNIPER CURED SALMON

SERVES 6–8

10 juniper berries

2 tablespoons sea salt flakes

80 g (2¾ oz/1⅓ cups) chopped dill

grated zest of 1 lime

2 teaspoons ground black pepper

3 tablespoons vodka

3 teaspoons caster (superfine) sugar

500 g (1 lb 2 oz) boneless, skinless
salmon fillet

MUSTARD AND DILL SAUCE

1 tablespoon dijon mustard

1 teaspoon caster (superfine) sugar

100 ml (3½ fl oz) sunflower oil

2 teaspoons white wine vinegar

2 tablespoons chopped dill

rye bread, to serve

1 **Roughly crush the juniper berries** using a mortar and pestle or spice grinder. In a shallow non-metallic dish, combine salt, dill, juniper, lime zest, pepper, vodka and sugar. Spread the mixture evenly in the dish, then lay the salmon in the dish and cover it with plastic wrap. Top the salmon with a slightly smaller dish filled with a heavy weight and refrigerate for 2 days, turning the salmon over every 12 hours.

2 **Combine mustard** and sugar in a bowl and gradually whisk in the oil until combined. Stir in the vinegar, dill and 1 tablespoon of boiling water and season to taste.

3 **Remove the salmon** from the marinade. Rinse under cold water to remove excess marinade and pat dry. Using a sharp knife, cut the salmon into thin slices.

4 **Drizzle the salmon** with the mustard and dill sauce and serve with rye bread.

SARDINES WITH CHERMOULA STUFFING

SERVES 4

105 g (3½ oz/1⅓ cups) fresh breadcrumbs

¼ preserved lemon, pith removed, washed and finely chopped (see Note)

6 green olives, pitted and finely chopped

½ red chilli, deseeded and finely chopped

1½ tablespoons chermoula paste

16 sardine fillets

olive oil, for drizzling

lemon wedges, to serve

1   Preheat the oven to 200°C (400°F/Gas 6). Lightly grease a large ovenproof dish. Set aside 25 g (1 oz/⅓ cup) of the breadcrumbs. In a bowl, combine the remaining breadcrumbs, the preserved lemon, olives, chilli and chermoula paste and mix well.

2   Lay eight of the sardine fillets, in a single layer, skin side down, in the dish. Divide a generous layer of the chermoula stuffing over the sardines. Lay the remaining eight sardines, skin side up, on top. Lightly scatter each with the reserved breadcrumbs and drizzle with olive oil.

3   Cover the dish with foil. Bake for 15 minutes. Remove the foil and bake for a further 10 minutes, or until cooked and golden. Serve immediately with lemon wedges.

Note: Preserved lemons (sold in jars) and chermoula paste are available from supermarkets and delicatessens.

TUNA & CANNELLINI BEAN PATE

SERVES 4–6

150 g (5½ oz/¾ cup) cannellini beans, soaked in water overnight, drained

1 bay leaf

2 x 150 g (5½ oz) tuna steaks

150 ml (5 fl oz) garlic-infused olive oil, plus extra, to serve

½ small red onion, finely chopped

3 tablespoons finely chopped flat-leaf (Italian) parsley

1 tablespoon chopped thyme

2 teaspoons lemon zest

2 tablespoons lemon juice

sea salt, to taste

GARLIC CROSTINI

1 loaf pide (Turkish/flat bread)

3 tablespoons garlic-infused olive oil

1 Put the cannellini beans, bay leaf and 625 ml (21½ fl oz/2½ cups) of water in a saucepan over high heat and bring to the boil. Reduce the heat and simmer, covered, for 1 hour, or until the beans are tender but not falling apart. Drain the beans into a colander and rinse with cold water. Discard the bay leaf.

2 Meanwhile, put the tuna steaks on a plate and place in a 30 cm (12 inch) steamer. Cover with a lid and sit the steamer over a saucepan or wok of boiling water. Steam for 4–5 minutes, or until the tuna is almost cooked but is still pink in the centre. Remove the tuna from the steamer and drizzle with 3 tablespoons of garlic-infused olive oil. Cool to room temperature, then flake the flesh with a fork.

3 Put the onion, parsley, thyme, lemon zest, lemon juice, sea salt and freshly ground black pepper in a large bowl and add the cannellini beans. With the back of a fork gently crush the beans, then add the tuna and remaining oil and toss gently to combine. Spoon the pâté into small bowls, garnish with freshly ground black pepper and drizzle with a little extra garlic oil.

4 Preheat the oven to 160°C (315°F/Gas 2–3) and line two baking trays with baking paper. Cut the bread into 1 cm (½ inch) thick slices. Lightly brush each side of the bread with the garlic oil, then arrange on the baking trays. Bake for 15 minutes, or until lightly golden brown, then turn over and bake for a further 15 minutes. Allow the crostini to cool, then serve with the pâté.

CARAMEL PRAWNS

SERVES 4

1 tablespoon peanut oil

24 raw king prawns (shrimp), peeled and deveined, tails intact

2 garlic cloves, crushed

3 red Asian shallots, finely chopped

60 g (2¼ oz/⅓ cup) grated palm sugar (jaggery) or soft brown sugar

2 tablespoons fish sauce

2 tablespoons rice vinegar

2 tablespoons chopped coriander (cilantro) leaves

lime wedges, to serve (optional)

1 Heat a wok over high heat, add the oil and swirl to coat. Add the prawns, garlic and shallots and stir-fry for about 1 minute, or until the prawns just start turning pink. Remove and set aside.

2 Put the sugar, fish sauce and vinegar in the wok with 125 ml (4 fl oz/½ cup) of water and boil for 5–10 minutes, or until reduced and syrupy. Return the prawns to the wok and stir-fry for 1–2 minutes, or until they are cooked through and coated with the caramel sauce. Stir in the coriander and serve with lime wedges, if desired.

PRAWN BANANA LEAF CUPS

MAKES 8

16 x 10 cm (4 inch) circles of banana leaf

300 g (10½ oz) raw prawns (shrimp), peeled and deveined

1 small red chilli, seeded

2 teaspoons Thai red curry paste

3 cm (1¼ inch) piece of lemongrass, white part only, roughly chopped

1 large egg

3 tablespoons coconut cream

1 tablespoon fish sauce

¼ teaspoon sugar

2 tablespoons unsalted peanuts

1 **Place two banana leaf circles** together to make a double layer. Make four small tucks around the circle, stapling them to secure as you go, to create a banana leaf 'cup'. Repeat to make eight cups in all. Alternatively you can use eight 100 ml (3½ fl oz) ramekins and cut out eight 7 cm (2¾ inch) rounds of baking paper.

2 **Tip the prawns** into a food processor with the chilli, curry paste, lemongrass, egg, coconut cream, fish sauce, sugar and half the peanuts. Blend to a rough paste.

3 **Evenly divide the mixture** among the cups or ramekins, then place a round of baking paper on top of each one. Arrange in a single layer in a steamer (you may need to do this in batches) and cover with a lid. Sit the steamer over a wok or saucepan of simmering water and steam for 10–12 minutes, or until the mixture has risen and feels firm to the touch. Remove the baking paper.

4 **Meanwhile,** lightly toast the remaining peanuts. Cool a little, then roughly chop. Scatter over the prawn cups and serve.

SCALLOPS IN BLACK BEAN SAUCE

SERVES 4

2 tablespoons oil

32 scallops, rinsed and drained very
well, roe discarded

1 tablespoon salted fermented black
beans

1 tablespoon soy sauce

2 tablespoons Chinese rice wine

1 teaspoon sugar

1 garlic clove, finely chopped

1 spring onion (scallion), finely chopped

½ teaspoon finely grated fresh ginger

1 teaspoon sesame oil

1 spring onion (scallion), extra, thinly
sliced on the diagonal

1 Heat 1 tablespoon of the oil in a wok and swirl to coat. When hot, add the scallops (in batches if necessary) and cook over high heat for 2 minutes, or until firm. Transfer to a plate and drain to remove any excess liquid.

2 Wash the black beans thoroughly under cold running water. Mix together the soy sauce, rice wine, sugar and 1 tablespoon of water in a cup.

3 Add the remaining oil to the wok and heat until it begins to smoke. Add the garlic, spring onion and ginger and cook for 30 seconds. Add the beans and the soy sauce mixture and bring to the boil.

4 Return the scallops to the sauce with the sesame oil and simmer for 30 seconds. Serve immediately, garnished with the extra spring onion.

GARLIC CHILLI PRAWNS

SERVES 4

1 tablespoon peanut oil

24 raw king prawns (shrimp), peeled and deveined, tails intact

2 garlic cloves, finely chopped

1 small red chilli, seeded and finely chopped

1–2 tablespoons chilli garlic sauce

2 teaspoons dark soy sauce

sesame oil, for drizzling

2 spring onions (scallions), green part only, cut diagonally into 3 cm (1¼ inch) lengths, to garnish

1 **Heat a wok** over high heat, add the oil and swirl to coat. Add the prawns and the garlic and stir-fry for 1 minute, or until the prawns turn pink.

2 **Add the chilli,** chilli garlic sauce and soy sauce and stir-fry for a further 2 minutes, or until the prawns are curled and glazed with the sauce. Drizzle with sesame oil, garnish with spring onion and serve.

CLAMS IN YELLOW BEAN SAUCE

SERVES 4

1.5 kg (3 lb 5 oz) clams (vongole)
1 tablespoon oil
2 garlic cloves, crushed
1 tablespoon grated fresh ginger
2 tablespoons yellow bean sauce (taucheo)
125 ml (4 fl oz/½ cup) chicken stock
1 spring onion (scallion), finely chopped

1 **Wash the clams** in several changes of cold water, leaving them for a few minutes each time to remove any grit. Scrub the clams well, discarding any that remain open. Drain well.

2 **Heat the wok** until very hot, add the oil and stir-fry the garlic and ginger for 30 seconds. Add the yellow bean sauce and clams, and toss together.

3 **Add the stock** and stir until the clams have all opened, discarding any that do not open after 3 minutes. Season with salt and white pepper.

4 **Transfer the clams** to a plate, garnish with the spring onion and serve.

TEMPURA PRAWNS AND VEGETABLES

SERVES 4

TEMPURA BATTER

60 g (2¼ oz/½ cup) plain (all-purpose) flour

60 g (2¼ oz/½ cup) cornflour (cornstarch)

1 teaspoon baking powder

¼ teaspoon salt

about 185 ml (6 fl oz/¾ cup) cold water, mixed with 4–6 ice cubes

16 raw king prawns (shrimp), peeled and deveined, tails intact

5 asparagus spears, trimmed and sliced in half on the diagonal

½ small orange sweet potato, peeled and thinly sliced

1 red capsicum (pepper), cut into 2 cm (¾ inch) wedges

2 slender eggplants (aubergines), thinly sliced on the diagonal

4 large fresh shiitake mushrooms, cut in half

vegetable oil, for deep-frying

ready-made tempura dipping sauce, to serve

wasabi paste, to serve

1 You will need to make up two separate quantities of the tempura batter because it thickens on use. Use one quantity of batter first, then mix the second batch later as it is needed. The batter is best made as close as possible to cooking time, so ensure the other ingredients are prepared beforehand.

2 To make the batter, divide the flour, cornflour, baking powder and salt between two bowls and mix well. To one bowl add enough water, with half the ice cubes, to make up a thin batter — you will need about 90 ml (3 fl oz) per batch. Mix lightly with chopsticks for about 30 seconds. The mixture should still be very lumpy with the flour not quite mixed through.

3 Fill a wok one-third full of oil and heat to 180°C (350°F), or until a cube of bread dropped in the oil browns in 15 seconds. Working in batches, dip the prawns and vegetables lightly into the batter and cook until lacy, crisp and golden. Remove from the wok with a spider and drain on crumpled paper towels. When the batter becomes too thick, make up the second batch and use it straight away. Continue cooking the remaining prawns and vegetables, making sure the oil stays at 180°C (350°F) to ensure a crisp batter.

4 Serve on a large platter with some tempura dipping sauce and wasabi paste.

PRAWN TOASTS

MAKES 12

250 g (9 oz) prawn (shrimp) meat

2 spring onions (scallions), finely chopped

2 garlic cloves, crushed

1 stem lemongrass, white part only, finely chopped

1 large handful coriander (cilantro) leaves, chopped

1 egg, lightly beaten

2 teaspoons fish sauce

6 slices day-old sliced white bread, crusts removed

vegetable oil, for deep-frying

12 coriander (cilantro) leaves, extra

1 Process the prawns in a food processor until finely chopped. Transfer to a bowl, add the spring onion, garlic, lemongrass and coriander and mix well. Stir in the egg and fish sauce to form a paste. Cover and refrigerate for at least 30 minutes.

2 Spread the paste evenly and thickly over the bread. Cut the bread in half into rectangles or triangles.

3 Fill a wok one-third full of oil and heat to 180°C (350°F), or until a cube of bread dropped in the oil browns in 15 seconds. Add a few bread slices at a time, paste-side-down, and cook for 1–2 minutes. Turn over and cook for a further minute, or until golden. Drain on crumpled paper towels. Garnish each toast with a coriander leaf and serve warm.

SUGAR CANE PRAWNS

MAKES 8

DIPPING SAUCE

4 tablespoons fish sauce

1 small red chilli, sliced

1 tablespoon toasted peanuts, finely chopped

2 teaspoons sugar

1 teaspoon chopped coriander (cilantro) leaves

650 g (1 lb 7 oz) raw king prawns (shrimp), peeled and deveined

1 egg white

2 tablespoons coriander (cilantro) leaves, chopped

1 spring onion (scallion), finely chopped

2 garlic cloves, chopped

2 teaspoons fish sauce

8 pieces of sugar cane, about 10 cm (4 inches) long and about 1–2 cm (½–¾ inch) wide (see Note)

oil, for deep-frying

1 **To make the dipping sauce**, combine the fish sauce, chilli, chopped peanuts, sugar, coriander and 1 tablespoon of water in small bowl. Mix to dissolve the sugar, then set aside until ready to serve.

2 **Put the prawns** in a food processor and process until well chopped. Add the egg white and mix well. Transfer the mixture to a bowl and add the coriander, spring onion, garlic and fish sauce.

3 **Divide the mixture** into eight and, with slightly wet hands, mould a portion around the sugar cane, covering about two-thirds of the stick. Repeat with the remaining mixture and arrange on a lined baking tray.

4 **Fill a wok** one-third full of oil and heat to 190°C (375°F), or until a cube of bread dropped in the oil browns in 10 seconds. Add the sugar cane prawns in batches and cook for 4–5 minutes, or until they are golden brown and slightly puffed, turning once during cooking. Drain on crumpled paper towels and serve hot with the dipping sauce.

Note: To get the most out of these, bite off some prawn, then suck on the sweet sugar cane. Tinned sugar cane is available from Asian food stores. Cut the pieces into half thicknesses, then chop to 10 cm (4 inch) lengths.

SMOKED TROUT PATE

SERVES 6

2 whole smoked trout or 4 smoked
    trout fillets, skinned

200 g (7 oz) cream cheese

2 tablespoons finely chopped dill

juice of ½ lemon

pinch of cayenne pepper

toast, for serving

lemon wedges, for serving

1 If using whole fish, skin the smoked trout, remove the heads and skin, then lift the flesh off the bones.

2 Break the flesh into flakes and put in a bowl or food processor. Either mash the flesh with a fork or briefly process until it is broken up, but still with plenty of texture.

3 Beat the cream cheese with a wooden spoon until soft. Add the smoked trout flesh and mix everything together well. Stir in the dill and lemon juice, then season with salt, pepper and cayenne pepper.

4 Chill the pâté until you need it but bring it to room temperature before serving or the cream cheese may cause it to go too solid. Serve with Melba or brown toast. Provide extra lemon wedges to squeeze over.

CRAB CAKES WITH AVOCADO SALSA

SERVES 4

350 g (12 oz) fresh crabmeat or tinned crabmeat

2 eggs, lightly beaten

1 spring onion (scallion), finely chopped

1 tablespoon mayonnaise

2 teaspoons sweet chilli sauce

100 g (4 oz/1¼ cups) fresh white breadcrumbs

oil, for shallow-frying

plain (all-purpose) flour, for dusting

lime wedges, for serving

AVOCADO SALSA

2 ripe roma (plum) tomatoes, chopped

1 small red onion, finely chopped

1 large ripe avocado, diced

60 ml (2 fl oz/¼ cup) lime juice

2 tablespoons chervil leaves

½ teaspoon caster (superfine) sugar

1 **Pick over the crabmeat** and pull out any stray pieces of shell or cartilage.

2 **Combine the crabmeat,** eggs, spring onion, mayonnaise, sweet chilli sauce and breadcrumbs in a bowl, season with salt and freshly ground black pepper, then stir well.

3 **Using wet hands,** form the crab mixture into eight small flat patties. Cover and put in the fridge for 30 minutes.

4 **For the avocado salsa,** put the tomato, onion, avocado, lime juice, chervil leaves and sugar in a bowl. Season to taste with salt and freshly ground black pepper, and toss gently to combine.

5 **Heat the oil** in a large frying pan over medium heat. Dust the crab cakes with flour and cook for 3 minutes on each side, or until golden brown—only turn them once so they don't break up. Drain on crumpled paper towels.

6 **Serve** the crab cakes with the avocado salsa and lime wedges.

DEEP-FRIED PACIFIC OYSTERS WITH DIPPING SAUCE

SERVES 4

24 Pacific oysters or any other large oyster on the shell

30 g (1 oz/¼ cup) plain (all-purpose) flour

1 egg, mixed with 3 teaspoons cold water

60 g (2¼ oz/1 cup) panko (Japanese breadcrumbs) or dry packaged breadcrumbs

vegetable oil, for deep-frying

SWEET THAI DIPPING SAUCE

4 tablespoons white wine vinegar

2½ tablespoons caster (superfine) sugar

1 slice fresh ginger

1 Lebanese (short) cucumber, seeded and finely diced

1 small red chilli, seeded and sliced

1 tablespoon chopped coriander (cilantro) leaves

1 **Remove the oysters** from their shells and lightly coat in the flour. Wash the shells, removing any grit from them, then dry well and set aside for later. Coat the oysters in the egg mixture and then the panko, pressing on firmly. Arrange the oysters on a plate, cover and refrigerate for at least 30 minutes.

2 **To make the dipping sauce,** put the vinegar, sugar and ginger in a small saucepan and heat to dissolve the sugar. Bring to the boil, then remove from the heat and allow to cool to room temperature. Discard the ginger and stir in the cucumber, chilli and coriander.

3 **Fill a wok** one-third full of oil to 180°C (350°F), or until a cube of bread dropped in the oil browns in 15 seconds. Deep-fry the oysters in batches for 1 minute, or until golden brown. Remove from the oil with a slotted spoon and drain on crumpled paper towels. Put the oysters back in the shells and drizzle with the dipping sauce or, if you prefer, serve the sauce in a bowl on the side.

SCALLOPS WITH SAFFRON BUTTER

SERVES 6

SAFFRON BUTTER
200 g (7 oz) butter, softened
½ teaspoon saffron threads
1 tablespoon lime juice

CUCUMBER SALAD
2 Lebanese (short) cucumbers, peeled
1 tablespoon chopped dill
1 tablespoon lime juice
2 teaspoons extra virgin olive oil

24 scallops, roe attached in their shell

1 Combine the butter, saffron threads, lime juice and salt and pepper in a bowl. Roll into a thin log, wrap in foil and refrigerate until required.

2 To make the cucumber salad, peel the cucumber flesh into fine strips lengthways using a vegetable peeler, avoiding the seeds. In a bowl, mix together the cucumber, dill, lime juice, oil and season to taste with salt and pepper.

3 Place the scallops onto a baking tray and top each one with a thin slice of the saffron butter. Cook under a hot grill (broiler) for 4–5 minutes, or until the butter has melted and the scallops are lightly golden.

4 Place the cucumber salad onto the centre of each serving plate and arrange the scallops around the salad.

THAI-STYLE MUSSELS IN AROMATIC COCONUT SAUCE

SERVES 4

1 kg (2 lb 4 oz) black mussels (about 40 mussels)

1 stem lemongrass, chopped into 2 cm (¾ inch) pieces

2 kaffir lime leaves, torn

1 tablespoon vegetable oil

1 red onion, finely chopped

2 garlic cloves, finely chopped

1 tablespoon red curry paste

270 ml (9½ fl oz) tin coconut milk

1 tablespoon fish sauce

1 tablespoon lime juice

2 teaspoons grated palm sugar (jaggery) or soft brown sugar

1 long red chilli, cut into thin strips

2 kaffir lime leaves, extra, shredded

1 Scrub the mussels clean and remove the beards. Discard any opened mussels that do not close when tapped on the work surface. Bring 750 ml (26 fl oz/3 cups) of water to the boil in a large saucepan and stir in the lemongrass and lime leaves. Add the mussels and cook, covered, for 2–3 minutes, or until the mussels have opened. Discard any unopened ones. Remove the mussels from the cooking liquid using a slotted spoon.

2 Meanwhile, heat the oil in a large wok. Add the onion and garlic and stir-fry for 2 minutes, or until softened. Add the curry paste and stir-fry for 1 minute, then stir in the coconut milk. Bring the sauce to the boil, then reduce the heat and simmer for 3 minutes. Add the fish sauce, lime juice and palm sugar.

3 Arrange the mussels in serving bowls, pour the sauce over the top and garnish with strips of chilli and shredded lime leaves.

HAR GOW DUMPLINGS

MAKES 24

FILLING

500 g (1 lb 2 oz) raw prawns (shrimp), peeled and deveined

45 g (1½ oz) pork or bacon fat (rind removed), finely diced

40 g (1½ oz) finely chopped bamboo shoots

1 spring onion (scallion), finely chopped

1 teaspoon sugar

3 teaspoons soy sauce

½ teaspoon roasted sesame oil

1 egg white, lightly beaten

1 teaspoon salt

1 tablespoon cornflour (cornstarch)

24 gow gee wrappers (8–9 cm/3¼–3½ inches)

soy sauce or hot chilli sauce, to serve

1 To make the filling, cut half the prawns into 1 cm (½ inch) chunks, then chop the remaining prawns using a knife or food processor until finely minced. Combine all the prawns in a large bowl. Add the pork fat, bamboo shoots, spring onion, sugar, soy sauce, sesame oil, egg white, salt and cornflour. Mix well.

2 Put 1 teaspoon of the filling in the centre of each gow gee wrapper and fold the wrapper over to make a half-moon shape. Spread a little water along the edge of the wrapper and use your thumb and index finger to form small pleats along the outside edge. With the other hand, press the two opposite edges together to seal. The inside edge should curve in a semicircle to conform to the shape of the pleated edge.

3 Line two bamboo steamers with baking paper and punch with holes. Put the dumplings in the steamers and cover to prevent them drying out while you work.

4 When you are ready to cook the har gow, sit the steamers over a wok of simmering water and steam, covered, for 6–8 minutes, or until the wrappers are translucent. Reverse the steamers halfway through cooking. Serve with soy or hot chilli sauce.

Note: Shaping the har gow takes a little practice — don't overfill them or the filling will leak out and they won't fold or stick properly.

STEAMED OYSTERS WITH HOT SESAME OIL

SERVES 4

rock salt, for lining

24 shucked oysters

3 spring onions (scallions), trimmed and cut into 5 cm (2 inch) matchsticks

1 long red chilli, seeded and cut into very thin strips

3 teaspoons finely grated fresh ginger

1 tablespoon light soy sauce

1 tablespoon roughly chopped coriander (cilantro) leaves (optional)

1 tablespoon sesame oil

1 **Fill a wok** one-third full of water and bring to simmering point. Take a plate that fits in your steamer basket (with sufficient space around it for you to remove the plate when it is hot) and line the plate with rock salt.

2 **Arrange a single layer** of oysters on top of the salt — this will prevent them sliding around. Put some spring onion, chilli and ginger on each oyster and drizzle with a little soy sauce.

3 **Cover and steam** over the wok of simmering water for 2 minutes. Repeat with the remaining oysters, scattering with a little coriander when steamed.

4 **Put the sesame oil** in a small saucepan and heat briefly over high heat. Drizzle the oil over the oysters and serve immediately.

STEAMED CRABMEAT IN RAMEKINS

SERVES 4

2 x 170 g (6 oz) tins crabmeat
(or 350 g/12 oz fresh)

300 g (10½ oz) white boneless fish
fillets, chopped

140 g (5 oz) tin coconut milk

1 stem lemongrass, white part only,
finely chopped

2 spring onions (scallions), finely
chopped

1 tablespoon fish sauce

1 teaspoon lime juice

1 teaspoon grated palm sugar (jaggery)
or soft brown sugar

2 eggs, separated

3 tablespoons chopped coriander
(cilantro) leaves

4 kaffir lime leaves

1 **Drain the crabmeat,** then squeeze dry with your hands. Set aside.

2 **Pat the fish** pieces dry with paper towels and put in a food processor with the coconut milk, lemongrass, spring onion, fish sauce, lime juice, palm sugar and the egg yolks. Process until smooth, then transfer to a bowl and fold in the crabmeat and coriander.

3 **Beat the egg whites** to soft peaks, then fold into the fish mixture. Spoon into four 185 ml (6 fl oz/¾ cup) ramekins and smooth the surface. Top each ramekin with a lime leaf.

4 **Evenly space the ramekins** in a large bamboo steamer. Sit the steamer over a wok of simmering water and steam, covered, for 20 minutes, or until cooked through. Serve warm or cold.

OYSTERS ROCKEFELLER

MAKES 24

24 oysters on the half-shell

rock salt, for stacking

60 g (2¼ oz) butter

2 slices bacon, finely chopped

8 English spinach leaves, finely chopped

2 spring onions (scallions), finely chopped

2 tablespoons finely chopped flat-leaf (Italian) parsley

4 tablespoons dry breadcrumbs

dash of Tabasco sauce

1 **Arrange the oysters** in their shells on a bed of rock salt in a baking tray — the salt will hold the oysters steady and stop the filling falling out later during grilling. Cover and refrigerate until needed.

2 **Heat the grill** (broiler) to high.

3 **Meanwhile,** melt the butter in a frying pan, then add bacon and cook over medium heat for about 2 minutes, or until browned. Add the spinach, spring onion, parsley, breadcrumbs and a dash of Tabasco and cook for about 1 minute, or until the spinach has wilted.

4 **Spoon the mixture** onto the oysters and grill for 2–3 minutes, or until the topping is golden. Serve immediately, while hot.

HONEY AND LIME PRAWN KEBABS WITH MANGO SALSA

SERVES 4

3 tablespoons clear runny honey

1 small red chilli, seeded and finely chopped

2 tablespoons olive oil

grated zest and juice of 2 limes

1 large garlic clove, crushed

2 cm (¾ inch) piece fresh ginger, peeled and finely grated

1 tablespoon chopped coriander (cilantro) leaves

32 tiger or king prawns (shrimp), peeled and deveined, tails intact

MANGO SALSA

2 tomatoes

1 small just-ripe mango, diced

½ small red onion, diced

1 small red chilli, seeded and finely chopped

grated zest and juice of 1 lime

2 tablespoons chopped coriander (cilantro) leaves

1 **In a small bowl,** whisk together the honey, chilli, oil, lime zest and lime juice, garlic, ginger and coriander. Place prawns in a non-metallic dish, add the marinade and toss well. Cover and refrigerate for several hours, turning the prawns occasionally.

2 **Before you start cooking,** soak eight bamboo skewers in cold water for 30 minutes. While skewers are soaking, make the salsa. Score a cross in the base of each tomato and put them in a heatproof bowl. Cover with boiling water, leave for 30 seconds, then plunge them in cold water and peel the skin away from the cross. Remove the seeds, dice the flesh, saving any juices, and put the tomato with all its juices in a bowl. Mix in the mango, onion, chilli, lime zest, lime juice and coriander.

3 **Heat the grill** (broiler) to high. Thread 4 prawns onto each skewer and grill for 4 minutes, or until pink and cooked through, turning halfway through cooking and basting regularly with the leftover marinade. Serve at once with the salsa.

Note: When threading the prawns on the skewers, don't squash them too closely together as they may not cook through properly.

SNAPPER, SCALLOP AND DILL TERRINE

SERVES 12

60 g (2 oz) butter
500 g (1 lb 2 oz) skinless snapper fillets or other firm white fish
12 large scallops
250 g (9 oz/1 cup) cottage cheese
1 tablespoon lemon juice
2 eggs
2 egg whites
3 tablespoons chopped dill
1 small handful dill sprigs, to serve
2–3 tablespoons pink salmon roe, to serve
½ baguette, thinly sliced, to serve

1 **Preheat the oven** to 170°C (325°F/Gas 3). Lightly spray a 1 litre (35 fl oz/4 cup) capacity loaf (bar) tin with oil and line with baking paper.

2 **Melt the butter** in a large frying pan, add the snapper and fry gently for 3 minutes. Add the scallops and cook for 2 minutes, turning them halfway through. Remove the pan from the heat and set aside to cool.

3 **Transfer the cooled seafood** to a processor fitted with the metal blade and add the cottage cheese, lemon juice, eggs and egg whites. Whizz for 12 seconds, or until smooth. Add the chopped dill and whizz in 3-second bursts for 9–12 seconds, or until the mixture is flecked with green.

4 **Carefully spread the mixture** into the prepared tin and put the loaf tin in a roasting tin. Pour in enough boiling water to come halfway up the sides of the tin and bake for 45–50 minutes, or until the terrine is firm and a skewer inserted into the centre comes out clean.

5 **Leave the terrine** in the water until cold, then remove from the water, cover with plastic wrap and chill for 2 hours.

6 **Briefly dip the tin** in hot water and invert the terrine onto a board. Garnish with the dill sprigs and salmon roe. Cut into slices to serve.

SCALLOPS WITH LIME AND GINGER BUTTER

SERVES 4

75 g (2½ oz) unsalted butter

6 kaffir lime leaves, finely chopped

1 teaspoon finely grated fresh ginger

1 teaspoon finely chopped lemongrass, white part only

1 teaspoon fish sauce

16 cleaned scallops, on the half-shell

1 **Preheat a barbecue flat plate** or grill plate to medium. Melt the butter in a small saucepan on the stovetop over low heat. Remove from the heat and stir in the lime leaves, ginger, lemongrass and fish sauce. Cover and keep warm.

2 **Remove the scallops** from their shells — you may need to use a small, sharp knife to slice them free, being careful not to leave any scallop meat behind. Rinse the scallops, pat them dry with paper towels and place in a bowl with half the butter mixture. Mix gently to coat the scallops.

3 **Wipe the scallop shells** with a clean, damp cloth and put them on the edge of the barbecue to warm through. When warm, arrange the shells on four serving plates.

4 **Sear the scallops** on the hotplate for 40–60 seconds on each side, or until golden and just cooked through. Quickly transfer to the warm shells and drizzle with the remaining butter mixture. Serve immediately.

MUSSELS WITH DILL AND CAPERS

SERVES 4

125 ml (4 fl oz/½ cup) cream

zest of 1 lemon

4 tablespoons dill sprigs

2 tablespoons baby capers, rinsed and drained

10 pitted black olives

1 kg (2 lb 4 oz) black mussels, scrubbed, beards removed

3 tablespoons white wine

2 garlic cloves, crushed

70 g (2½ oz) butter, chopped

4 spring onions (scallions), finely sliced

1 **Preheat a kettle** or covered barbecue to medium direct heat. Combine the cream, lemon zest, dill, capers and olives.

2 **Put the mussels** in a frying pan on the barbecue, pour the wine over and lower the lid. Cook for 1–2 minutes, or until the mussels start to open.

3 **Add the garlic** and butter, and toss them through the mussels using tongs. Pour the cream and dill mixture over the mussels, then cover and cook for another minute, or until the mussels fully open. Toss to coat the mussels in the sauce, then discard any unopened mussels. Serve warm, sprinkled with the spring onion.

DEEP-FRIED PRAWN BALLS WITH ASIAN GREENS

SERVES 4

PRAWN BALLS

350 g (12 oz) raw prawn (shrimp) meat, chopped

80 g (2¾ oz/1 cup) fresh white breadcrumbs

2 spring onions (scallions), finely chopped

2 teaspoons grated fresh ginger

1 egg yolk

1 teaspoon cornflour (cornstarch)

vegetable oil, for deep-frying

1 tablespoon thinly sliced fresh ginger

100 g (3½ oz/1 cup) snowpeas (mangetout), topped and tailed

100 g (3½ oz) sugar snap peas, trimmed

500 g (1 lb 2 oz) baby bok choy (pak choy), trimmed, washed and quartered lengthways

2 tablespoons mirin

1 tablespoon oyster sauce

1 tablespoon sweet chilli sauce

1½ large handfuls coriander (cilantro) leaves

1   To make the prawn balls, process the prawn meat, breadcrumbs, spring onion, ginger, egg yolk and cornflour in a food processor until the mixture comes together. Using wet hands form into 12 golf ball-sized balls. Refrigerate for 20 minutes.

2   Fill a wok one-third full of vegetable oil. Heat to 180°C (350°F), or until a cube of bread dropped in the oil browns in 15 seconds. Cook the prawn balls a few at a time for 2–3 minutes, or until cooked through and golden. Remove with a slotted spoon. Drain on crumpled paper towels.

3   Pour off all but 1 tablespoon of oil from the wok. Heat, then add the ginger, snowpeas and sugar snap peas and stir-fry over high heat for 2 minutes. Add 3 tablespoons of water and stir in the bok choy. Cover the wok and steam, stirring occasionally, for 3–4 minutes, or until the vegetables are just tender.

4   Stir in the combined mirin, oyster sauce and sweet chilli sauce. Add the prawn balls and toss well. Garnish with coriander leaves and serve with jasmine rice.

RICE NOODLE ROLLS FILLED WITH PRAWNS

SERVES 4

SAUCE

140 g (5 oz/½ cup) sesame paste (see Note)

4 tablespoons light soy sauce

3 tablespoons lime juice

3 tablespoons grated palm sugar (jaggery) or soft brown sugar

1 tablespoon sesame oil

2 tablespoons peanut oil

1 teaspoon sesame oil

4 garlic cloves, finely chopped

5 spring onions (scallions), finely sliced

150 g (5½ oz/1 large bunch) garlic chives, cut into 2 cm (¾ inch) lengths

165 g (5¾ oz/1 cup) water chestnuts, finely sliced

3 tablespoons sesame seeds, lightly toasted

500 g (1 lb 2 oz) fresh rice sheet noodles

800 g (1 lb 12 oz) small raw prawns (shrimp), peeled and deveined

50 g (1¾ oz/⅓ cup) unsalted peanuts, crushed

1 **To make the sauce,** combine the sesame paste, soy sauce, lime juice, palm sugar and sesame oil in a bowl and stir until the sugar has dissolved and the sauce is smooth. Add a tablespoon of water if it's a little too thick.

2 **Heat the peanut oil** and sesame oil in a frying pan, add the garlic and cook for 1 minute. Add spring onion and garlic chives. Cook for about 2 minutes, or until softened. Add the water chestnuts and sesame seeds. Remove from the heat and allow to cool.

3 **Unroll the noodle sheets** and cut into eight 15 x 17 cm (6 x 6½ inch) pieces. Put 1 tablespoon of the chive mixture along one long end. Place four prawns, curled up, side by side, on top of the chive mixture and roll up the noodle sheet tightly, then sit it on a plate that fits inside a steamer. Repeat with the remaining rolls and filling ingredients. Lay the rolls side by side in two layers, with a layer of baking paper in between the rolls to stop them sticking together.

4 **Place the plate** in a steamer and cover with a lid. Sit the steamer over a wok or saucepan of simmering water and steam for 10 minutes, or until the prawns turn opaque and are cooked. Carefully lift the plate out of the steamer with a tea towel (dish towel) and drizzle some of the sauce over the top, and around the rolls, then sprinkle with the crushed peanuts. Serve extra sauce on the side.

Note: Sesame paste is a thick, brown paste made from sesame seeds. It is different from the Middle Eastern paste, tahini. It is available from Asian food stores.

PRAWN NORI ROLLS

MAKES 25 ROLLS

500 g (1 lb 2 oz) raw prawns (shrimp), peeled and deveined

1½ tablespoons fish sauce

1 tablespoon sake

2 tablespoons chopped coriander (cilantro) leaves

1 large kaffir lime leaf, finely shredded

1 tablespoon lime juice

2 teaspoons sweet chilli sauce

1 egg white, lightly beaten

5 sheets of nori

DIPPING SAUCE

3 tablespoons sake

3 tablespoons light soy sauce

1 tablespoon mirin

1 tablespoon lime juice

1 Put the prawns, fish sauce, sake, coriander, lime leaf, lime juice and sweet chilli sauce in a food processor and blend until smooth. Add the egg white and pulse for a few seconds to just combine.

2 Lay the nori sheets on a flat surface, shiny side down, and spread some prawn mixture over each sheet, leaving a 2 cm (¾ inch) border at one end. Roll up tightly, cover and refrigerate for 1 hour to firm. Using a sharp knife, trim the ends and cut into 2 cm (¾ inch) lengths.

3 Line a steamer with baking paper and punch with holes. Arrange the rolls in the steamer in a single layer and cover with a lid. Sit the steamer over a wok or saucepan of boiling water and steam for 5 minutes, or until cooked.

4 To make the dipping sauce, mix together all the ingredients in a small bowl. Serve with the nori rolls.

ASIAN OYSTERS

SERVES 4

12 oysters, on the shell

2 garlic cloves, finely chopped

2 x 2 cm (¾ x ¾ inch) piece ginger, finely sliced

2 spring onions (scallions), finely sliced on the diagonal

3 tablespoons Japanese soy sauce

3 tablespoons peanut oil

coriander (cilantro) leaves, to garnish

1   Line a large steamer with baking paper and punch with holes. Arrange the oysters in a single layer on top.

2   Put the garlic, ginger and spring onion in a bowl, mix together well, then sprinkle over the oysters.

3   Spoon 1 teaspoon of soy sauce over each oyster and cover the steamer with a lid. Sit the steamer over a wok or saucepan of simmering water and steam for about 2 minutes.

4   Heat the peanut oil in a small saucepan until smoking and carefully drizzle a little over each oyster. Garnish with the coriander leaves and serve immediately.

MOLLUSCS WITH WASABI BUTTER

SERVES 4–6

1.5 kg (3 lb 5 oz) pipis and/or clams (vongole)

24 black mussels

24 oysters, on the shell

lemon or lime wedges, to serve

WASABI BUTTER

250 g (9 oz) butter at room temperature, cut into cubes

3–4 tablespoons wasabi powder

2 tablespoons Japanese soy sauce

1 tablespoon chopped lime zest

2 tablespoons lime juice

2 tablespoons finely snipped chives

1 tablespoon finely chopped basil

1 tablespoon finely chopped coriander (cilantro) leaves

1 tablespoon finely chopped thyme

¼ teaspoon smoked paprika

1 To clean the pipis and clams, place them in a large bowl and cover with cold water. Leave them for 2–4 hours, changing the water every hour. This will remove any unwanted sand.

2 Scrub the mussels with a stiff brush and pull out the hairy beards. Discard any broken mussels, or open ones that don't close when tapped on the bench. Rinse well before steaming.

3 To make the wasabi butter, beat the butter with electric beaters until almost white. Fold in the remaining ingredients until well combined. Cover and refrigerate until using.

4 Put the oysters, mussels and strained pipis and clams in a double steamer in a single layer and cover with a lid. Sit the steamer over a wok or saucepan of boiling water and steam for 5–10 minutes, or until oysters are warmed through and the other molluscs have opened. Discard any unopened molluscs.

5 Melt the wasabi butter in a small saucepan over medium heat. Arrange the cooked molluscs on a large serving plate and drizzle with the wasabi butter.

6 Serve with lemon or lime wedges, a green salad and bread to soak up the buttery juices.

THAI FISH CAKES WITH GINGER & LIME DIPPING SAUCE

SERVES 4–6

FISH CAKES

500 g (1 lb 2 oz) skinless white fish
   fillets, roughly chopped

30 g (1 oz/¼ cup) cornflour (cornstarch)

2 tablespoons red curry paste

2 tablespoons fish sauce

1 egg, lightly beaten

3 spring onions (scallions), finely
   chopped

60 g (2 oz) green beans, thinly sliced

vegetable oil, for deep-frying

DIPPING SAUCE

1 large red chilli, seeded and chopped

2 garlic cloves, chopped

3 cm (1 inch) piece ginger, chopped

¼ small red onion, chopped

125 ml (4 fl oz/½ cup) lime juice

60 ml (2 fl oz/¼ cup) fish sauce

1 tablespoon shaved palm sugar
   (jaggery) or soft brown sugar

2 teaspoons light soy sauce

1 **To make the fish cakes,** put the fish in a processor fitted with the metal blade and whizz for 10 seconds. Add the cornflour, curry paste, fish sauce and egg. Whizz for 20 seconds, or until thoroughly combined. Transfer to a bowl and stir in the spring onion and beans. Using wet hands, form the mixture into twenty-four 4 cm (1½ inch) flat cakes. Refrigerate, uncovered, for at least 30 minutes to allow the fish cakes to dry out a little.

2 **Meanwhile,** to make the dipping sauce, put the chilli, garlic, ginger and red onion in a mini processor and whizz in short bursts for 15 seconds, or until thoroughly chopped. Add the lime juice, fish sauce, sugar and soy sauce. Whizz in short bursts until combined.

3 **Fill a deep-fryer** or large heavy-based saucepan one-third full of oil and heat to 180°C (350°F), or until a cube of bread dropped into the oil turns golden brown in 15 seconds. Fry the fish cakes in batches for 3–4 minutes, or until well browned and cooked through. Drain on paper towels. Serve the fish cakes with the dipping sauce.

SHELLFISH WITH FOAMING CITRUS BUTTER

MAKES 24

1 kg (2 lb 4 oz) live moreton bay bugs (flat head lobsters) (see Note)

sourdough or country-style bread, to serve

FOAMING CITRUS BUTTER

60 g (2 oz) butter

1 large garlic clove, crushed

1 tablespoon finely grated orange zest

1 tablespoon blood orange juice or regular orange juice

1 tablespoon lemon juice

1 tablespoon finely snipped chives

1 **Freeze the bugs** for 1–2 hours before cooking. Nearer to cooking time, heat the grill (broiler) to its highest setting.

2 **Plunge the semi-frozen bugs** into a large saucepan of boiling water for 2 minutes, then drain. Using a sharp knife or cleaver, cut each bug in half from head to tail. Put the bugs on a large baking tray, cut-side-up. Grill for 5–6 minutes, or until the flesh turns white and opaque, turning halfway through cooking.

3 **Meanwhile,** make the foaming citrus butter. Melt the butter in a small saucepan and when sizzling, add the garlic. Cook over medium heat for 1 minute, stirring. Stir in the orange zest, orange juice and lemon juice and bring to the boil. Add the chives and season with salt and pepper.

4 **Divide the bugs** among four serving plates, and serve the foaming citrus butter in small individual bowls for everyone to dip their shellfish and bread in. Finger bowls and napkins are also a good idea.

Note: Instead of moreton bay bugs (flat head lobsters) you could use live slipper lobsters or crayfish for this recipe. You may need to boil them for a slightly longer time to cook them, and you'll need to remove the heads before slicing them down the middle. Depending on their size, they may also need a little longer under the grill (broiler).

STEAMED SNAPPER FILLETS WITH CHILLI AND GARLIC OIL

SERVES 4

4 x 200 g (7 oz) snapper fillets, skin removed

3 tablespoons vegetable oil

1 tablespoon peanut oil

1 teaspoon toasted sesame oil

5 garlic cloves, very finely sliced

3 small red chillies, deseeded and finely sliced

½ teaspoon sea salt flakes

1 teaspoon finely grated fresh ginger

steamed Asian greens and rice, to serve

1 Bring a large saucepan or wok of water to the boil. Line a large bamboo steamer basket with baking paper and punch with holes. Put the snapper fillets over the top then cover with a lid. Put the steamer basket over the top of the boiling water, ensuring it fits snugly on the rim of the pan or wok. Cook for 7 minutes, or until the fish is opaque and flakes easily with a fork.

2 Meanwhile, put the vegetable, peanut and sesame oils in a small saucepan over a low heat. Add the garlic, chilli and the sea salt flakes and cook, stirring occasionally, for 8 minutes, or until lightly golden. Add the ginger and cook for a further 30 seconds, or until fragrant. Drizzle the oil over the fish and serve with steamed Asian greens and steamed rice.

SOUPS

SMOKED FISH CHOWDER

SERVES 4–6

500 ml (17 fl oz/2 cups) milk

500 g (1 lb 2 oz) smoked fish, trimmed and cut into large chunks

60 g (2 oz) butter

1 leek, white part only, roughly chopped

2 celery stalks, chopped

1 large carrot, chopped

2 garlic cloves, chopped

400 g (14 oz/3 medium) potatoes, cut into 5 cm (2 inch) pieces

1 teaspoon freshly grated nutmeg

500 ml (17 fl oz/2 cups) chicken stock or fish stock

125 ml (4 fl oz/½ cup) pouring cream

1 large handful flat-leaf (Italian) parsley, chopped

1 Heat the milk in a large deep saucepan. Add the fish and simmer for 8 minutes, or until the flesh flakes when tested. Transfer the fish to a plate and set aside to cool. Reserve the milk. Peel and discard the skin from the fish and roughly flake the flesh, removing any bones.

2 Heat the butter in a large heavy-based saucepan over medium–low heat. Add the leek, celery, carrot and garlic. Stir for 2 minutes to coat the vegetables in the butter. Reduce the heat, cover and sweat, stirring occasionally, for 5 minutes. Do not allow the vegetables to brown.

3 Add the chopped potato and nutmeg to the saucepan and stir to combine. Cook for 2 minutes, then add the stock. Bring to the boil, cover and cook for 20 minutes, or until the potato is tender. Set aside to cool slightly.

4 Using an immersion blender fitted with the chopping blade, whizz the soup for 10 seconds, or until roughly puréed. Stir in the fish, reserved milk, cream and parsley and gently reheat the soup. Season well with freshly ground black pepper.

Note: The soup will keep in the refrigerator, covered, for up to 3 days. It is not suitable for freezing.

GUMBO

SERVES 6

ROUX

80 ml (⅓ cup) oil
75 g (scant ⅔ cup) plain (all-purpose) flour
1 onion, finely chopped
1.5 litres (6 cups) boiling water

4 crabs, cleaned
450 g (1 lb) chorizo sausage, cut into bite-sized pieces
6 spring onions (scallions), sliced
1 green capsicum (pepper), roughly chopped
3 tablespoons chopped parsley
¼ teaspoon chilli powder
500 g (1 lb 2 oz) prawns (shrimp), peeled and deveined
24 oysters, shucked
½ teaspoon filé powder, optional (see Note)
1½ tablespoons long-grain rice

1 **To make the roux,** pour the oil into a large heavy-based saucepan on low heat. Gradually add the flour, stirring after each addition, to make a thin roux. Continue to cook and stir over a low heat for 35 minutes, or until it turns dark brown. Add the onion and cook for 4 minutes, or until tender. Gradually pour in the boiling water, continually stirring to dissolve the roux, and bring to a simmer.

2 **Cut the crabs** into small pieces. Add the crab, sausage, spring onion, capsicum, parsley and chilli powder to the roux. Cook for 30 minutes, then add the prawns and the oysters and their juices and cook for another 5 minutes, or until the prawns are pink. Season well with salt and pepper, then stir in the filé powder.

3 **Meanwhile,** cook the rice in salted boiling water for about 10 minutes, or until it is just cooked through. Ladle the gumbo into bowls, each containing a couple of tablespoons of rice in the bottom.

Note: Filé powder is a flavouring often used in Creole cooking. It is made by drying, then grinding sassafras leaves.

CRAB IN LIME AND LEMONGRASS BROTH

SERVES 4

1 tablespoon vegetable oil

1–2 teaspoons chilli paste in soy bean oil

4 red Asian shallots, finely chopped

1 garlic clove, finely chopped

200 g (7 oz) fresh crabmeat

1½ tablespoons fish sauce

1 litre (35 fl oz/4 cups) chicken stock

2 tablespoons lime juice

3 stems lemongrass, white part only, 1 bruised, 2 finely chopped

4 kaffir lime leaves, shredded

250 g (9 oz) asparagus, trimmed and cut into 3 cm (1¼ inch) lengths

1 tablespoon shredded coriander (cilantro) leaves, plus extra sprigs to serve

2 spring onions (scallions), thinly sliced

1 **Heat a wok** over medium heat, add the oil and swirl to coat. Stir-fry the chilli paste for about 30 seconds, or until fragrant. Add the shallots and garlic and stir-fry for 30 seconds, or until fragrant and just starting to brown. Stir in the crab meat and 3 teaspoons of fish sauce and stir-fry for 1 minute. Remove from the wok.

2 **Put the chicken stock**, lime juice, lemongrass, remaining fish sauce and three of the shredded lime leaves in a clean wok and heat until simmering. Simmer for 10 minutes, then strain to remove the lemongrass and lime leaves.

3 **Return the strained broth** to the wok and bring to the boil. Add the asparagus and cook for 2–3 minutes, or until tender but still firm. Add the crab mixture, stirring to combine well, and simmer for 1 minute, or until the crab is heated through. Remove from the heat and stir in the shredded coriander. Season with freshly ground black pepper.

4 **Serve** topped with coriander sprigs, spring onion and the remaining shredded lime leaf.

PUMPKIN, PRAWN AND COCONUT MILK SOUP

SERVES 4

CURRY PASTE

1 tablespoon oil

1 teaspoon tamarind concentrate

2 garlic cloves, chopped

4 red Asian shallots, chopped

5 white peppercorns

2 small red chillies

4 coriander (cilantro) roots

1 tablespoon chopped coriander
  (cilantro) stems

1 tablespoon chopped lemongrass

1 kg (2 lb 4 oz) raw prawns (shrimp)

1 tablespoon oil

1 onion, chopped

2 garlic cloves, chopped

1 carrot, chopped

2 tablespoons tomato paste
  (concentrated purée)

400 ml (14 fl oz) tin coconut cream

800 g (1 lb 12 oz) pumpkin, peeled and
  cut into 1.5 cm (⅝ inch) pieces

270 ml (9½ fl oz) tin coconut milk

1½ tablespoons fish sauce

1 tablespoon grated palm sugar
  (jaggery) or soft brown sugar

1 handful Thai basil

1   **To make the curry paste,** put all the ingredients in a small food processor or spice grinder and blend until smooth.

2   **Peel the prawns,** reserving the shells. Cut a slit down the back of the prawns and remove the vein.

3   **Heat a wok** over high heat, add the oil and swirl to coat. Cook the onion, garlic and carrot for 4–5 minutes, or until lightly coloured. Add the prawn shells and cook for 2–3 minutes, or until they turn orange. Add the tomato paste and 1 litre (35 fl oz/4 cups) of water, bring to the boil, then reduce the heat and simmer gently for 20 minutes. Don't boil the liquid, otherwise the prawn shells will make it bitter. Strain, reserving the liquid.

4   **Heat a clean wok** over high heat, add the paste and cook for 1–2 minutes, or until aromatic. Stir in the coconut cream and cook for 2 minutes. Add the reserved stock, pumpkin and coconut milk and cook for 5 minutes, or until the pumpkin is tender. Add the prawns and cook for 2 minutes, or until cooked. Stir in the fish sauce, palm sugar and basil and serve.

POTATO AND ANCHOVY CHOWDER WITH GARLIC PRAWNS

SERVES 4

GARLIC PRAWNS

2 garlic cloves, chopped

1 small red chilli, seeded and chopped

2 tablespoons chopped flat-leaf (Italian) parsley

1 tablespoon olive oil

16 raw prawns (shrimp), peeled and deveined

1 tablespoon olive oil

3 bacon slices, fat trimmed, chopped

1 onion, chopped

2 celery stalks, chopped

2 garlic cloves, chopped

80 g (2¾ oz) tin anchovies, drained

1 carrot, chopped

3 potatoes, about 400 g (14 oz), roughly chopped

375 ml (13 fl oz/1½ cups) chicken stock or fish stock

250 ml (9 fl oz/1 cup) milk

125 ml (4 fl oz/½ cup) pouring cream

3 tablespoons finely chopped flat-leaf (Italian) parsley

1 **To make the garlic prawns,** put the garlic, chilli and parsley in a mini processor and whizz for 15–20 seconds, or until finely chopped. With the motor running, add the oil and continue whizzing until the mixture forms a rough paste. Transfer to a bowl, add the prawns and toss to coat. Set aside to marinate for 30 minutes.

2 **Heat the oil** in a large heavy-based saucepan over medium–low heat. Add the bacon, onion, celery and garlic and cook, stirring, for 2 minutes. Reduce the heat, cover and simmer, stirring occasionally, for 5 minutes. Do not allow the bacon and vegetables to brown.

3 **Drain anchovies** on paper towels. Roughly chop and add to bacon mixture. Add carrot and potato. Stir to combine. Cook 2 minutes. Add stock and milk. Bring to the boil. Cook, covered, 15 minutes, or until the vegetables are tender.

4 **Remove the saucepan** from the heat. Using an immersion blender fitted with the chopping blade, whizz the soup for 20–30 seconds, or until smooth. Add the cream and most of the parsley, reserving some for garnish. Season well with freshly ground black pepper. Keep warm.

5 **Heat a large frying pan** over high heat and add the prawns and marinade all at once. Cook, turning, for 2 minutes, or until the prawns are just cooked through.

6 **Place a pile of prawns** in the centre of four large soup bowls and ladle the soup around the prawns. Sprinkle with the remaining parsley and serve immediately.

Note: The soup will keep in the refrigerator, covered, for up to 2 days. It is not suitable for freezing.

CLAMS WITH CORN AND BACON

SERVES 4

25 g (1 oz) butter

1 large onion, chopped

100 g (3½ oz) bacon, chopped

1.5 kg (3 lb 5 oz) fresh clams (vongole), cleaned (see Note)

1 large corn cob, kernels removed

150 ml (5 fl oz) dry alcoholic cider

150 ml (5 fl oz) fish stock

150 ml (5 fl oz) thick (double/heavy) cream

1 **Melt the butter** in a large saucepan over medium heat. Add the onion and bacon and cook for 5 minutes, or until the onion is soft and the bacon is cooked.

2 **Arrange the clams** in a single layer in a steamer and cover with a lid. Sit the steamer over a saucepan or wok of boiling water and steam for 8–10 minutes, or until the clams start to open. Discard any clams that have not opened.

3 **Add the corn kernels** to the onion and bacon and cook, stirring, for 3–4 minutes, or until tender.

4 **Pour in the cider** and fish stock, bring to the boil, then reduce the heat and simmer for 2 minutes. Stir in the cream, and season with salt and freshly ground black pepper.

5 **Tip in the clams** and toss them gently in the sauce. Serve in warmed deep bowls.

Note: If clams are unavailable, this recipe works just as well with pipis, cockles or mussels.

HEARTY SEAFOOD SOUP

SERVES 4

2 tablespoons dried shrimp

60 ml (2 fl oz/¼ cup) olive oil

1 large onion, finely chopped

3 garlic cloves, crushed

1 small red chilli, deseeded and finely chopped

1 teaspoon finely grated fresh ginger

3 tablespoons crunchy peanut butter

800 g (1 lb 12 oz) tinned chopped tomatoes

50 g (1¾ oz) creamed coconut, chopped (see Note)

400 ml (14 fl oz) coconut milk

generous pinch of ground cloves

4 tablespoons chopped coriander (cilantro) leaves

700 g (1 lb 9 oz) swordfish or other firm white fish, cut into large chunks

100 g (3½ oz) small prawns (shrimp), peeled and deveined

2 tablespoons chopped cashew nuts

1   Soak the dried shrimp in boiling water for 10 minutes, then drain.

2   Heat the oil in a deep saucepan and cook the onion gently for 5 minutes. Add the garlic, chilli and ginger and cook for 2 minutes. Stir in the dried shrimp, peanut butter, tomato, creamed coconut, coconut milk, ground cloves and half of the coriander. Bring the mixture to the boil and simmer gently for 10 minutes.

3   Remove from the heat, allow to cool a little, then tip the sauce into a food processor or blender and blend until thick and smooth. Alternatively, push the mixture through a coarse sieve or mouli by hand.

4   Return the sauce to the pan over medium heat. Add the swordfish and cook for 2 minutes, then add the prawns and continue to simmer until all the seafood is cooked — the prawns will be pink and the fish opaque. Serve with the cashews and remaining coriander sprinkled over the top.

Note: Creamed coconut is sold in a block. It needs to be chopped or grated and then stirred into a hot liquid. If you can't find it, use a 140 g (5 oz) tin of thick coconut cream. You can substitute the fish with marlin, tuna or monkfish.

TUNISIAN FISH SOUP

SERVES 6

60 ml (2 fl oz/¼ cup) olive oil

1 onion, chopped

1 celery stalk, chopped

4 garlic cloves, crushed

2 tablespoons tomato paste (concentrated purée)

1½ teaspoons ground turmeric

1½ teaspoons ground cumin

2 teaspoons harissa

1 litre (35 fl oz/4 cups) fish stock

2 bay leaves

200 g (7 oz/1 cup) orzo or other small pasta

500 g (1 lb 2 oz) mixed skinless snapper and sea bass fillets, cut into bite-sized chunks

2 tablespoons chopped mint, plus some extra leaves, for garnish

2 tablespoons lemon juice

1 **Heat the oil** in a large saucepan, add the onion and celery and cook for 8–10 minutes, or until softened. Add the garlic and cook for a further minute. Stir in the tomato paste, turmeric, cumin and harissa and cook, stirring constantly, for an extra 30 seconds.

2 **Pour the fish stock** into the saucepan and add the bay leaves. Bring the liquid to the boil, then reduce the heat to low and simmer gently for 15 minutes.

3 **Add the orzo** to the liquid and cook for 2–3 minutes, or until al dente. Drop the chunks of fish into the liquid and poach gently for 3–4 minutes, or until the fish is opaque. Stir in the mint and lemon juice, season to taste with salt, then serve with warm pitta bread. Garnish with mint leaves.

Note: You can substitute the fish with cod, haddock, ocean perch or coral trout.

RUSSIAN FISH SOUP

SERVES 4

50 g (1¾ oz) butter

1 large onion, thinly sliced

1 celery stalk, chopped

5 tablespoons plain (all-purpose) flour

2 tablespoons tomato paste
(concentrated purée)

1 litre (35 fl oz/4 cups) fish stock

2 large gherkins, rinsed and chopped

1 tablespoon capers, rinsed and
squeezed dry

1 bay leaf

¼ teaspoon freshly grated nutmeg

600 g (1 lb 5 oz) mixed white fish fillets,
skinned and cut into chunks

2 tablespoons chopped parsley

2 tablespoons chopped dill, plus a little
extra, for garnish

sour cream, for serving

1 **Melt the butter** in a large saucepan. Add the onion and celery and cook gently over low heat for 7–8 minutes, or until softened and translucent.

2 **Increase the heat,** stir in the flour and tomato paste and cook, stirring constantly, for 30 seconds. Pour in the fish stock and slowly bring to the boil, stirring frequently.

3 **Reduce the heat** to low and add the gherkins, capers, bay leaf, nutmeg and chunks of fish. Poach gently for 2–3 minutes, or until the fish is opaque. Gently stir in the parsley and dill and season generously with salt and pepper.

4 **Serve** each bowlful of soup topped with a spoonful of sour cream and a sprinkling of dill.

Note: You can substitute the fish with tench, haddock or sea bass.

SEAFOOD CHOWDER

SERVES 6

400 g (14 oz) smoked cod

750 ml (26 fl oz/3 cups) milk

400 g (14 oz) firm white fish fillets

3 boiling potatoes, cut into 1 cm
(½ inch) cubes

12 small raw prawns (shrimp), peeled
and deveined

3 tablespoons olive oil

3 leeks, white part only, finely chopped

2 garlic cloves, crushed

1 celery stalk, diced

1 carrot, diced

1 zucchini (courgette), diced

125 ml (4 fl oz/½ cup) dry white wine

2 litres (70 fl oz/8 cups) fish stock

2 bay leaves

60 g (2¼ oz) butter

100 g (3½ oz/heaped ¾ cup) plain
(all-purpose) flour

3 tablespoons chopped parsley

1 **Place the cod** on a plate with 125 ml (4 fl oz/½ cup) of the milk and cover with foil. Put the plate in a steamer and cover with a lid. Sit the steamer over a saucepan or wok of boiling water and steam for 10 minutes. Drain, reserving the milk.

2 **Wrap the fish fillets** in baking paper, place in the steamer and steam for 10 minutes. Break the cod and fish fillets into flakes. Steam the potatoes for 5 minutes, then add the prawns and steam for a further 3 minutes.

3 **Heat 1 tablespoon** of the oil in a saucepan over medium heat, add the leek, garlic, celery, carrot and zucchini and cook, stirring, for 3–4 minutes. Pour in the wine and cook for 5 minutes, or until the carrot has softened.

4 **Put the stock** and bay leaves in a large saucepan over high heat, bring to the boil, then reduce the heat and simmer for 10 minutes, or until the liquid has reduced by one-third, removing any scum that collects on the surface.

5 **Heat the butter** and remaining oil in a large saucepan over medium heat. Stir in the flour and cook for 1 minute. Remove from the heat and gradually whisk in the reserved steaming milk, reduced stock and remaining milk. Return to the heat and stir constantly until the mixture boils and thickens.

6 **Add the flaked fish,** prawns, potatoes and vegetable mixture and warm through. Season well, stir in the parsley and serve.

PRAWN LAKSA

SERVES 4–6

PASTE

1½ tablespoons coriander seeds

1 tablespoon cumin seeds

1 teaspoon ground turmeric

1 onion, roughly chopped

1 cm x 3 cm piece fresh ginger, peeled and roughly chopped

3 cloves garlic

3 stems lemongrass, white part only, sliced

6 macadamia nuts

4–6 small fresh red chillies

2–3 teaspoons shrimp paste

1 litre (35 fl oz/4 cups) chicken stock

60 ml (2 fl oz/¼ cup) oil

3 cups (750 ml) coconut milk

4 fresh kaffir lime leaves

2½ tablespoons lime juice

2 tablespoons fish sauce

2 tablespoons grated palm sugar (jaggery) or soft brown sugar

750 g raw medium prawns, peeled and deveined, with tails intact

250 g dried rice vermicelli noodles

1 cup (90 g) bean sprouts

4 fried tofu puffs, thinly sliced

3 tablespoons roughly chopped fresh Vietnamese mint

20 g (1 oz/⅔ cup) fresh coriander leaves

lime wedges, to serve

1 To make the paste, dry-roast the coriander seeds over medium heat for 1–2 minutes, or until fragrant, tossing constantly to prevent burning. Grind in a mortar and pestle or a spice grinder. Repeat with the cumin seeds. Place all the spices, onion, ginger, garlic, lemongrass, macadamias, chillies and shrimp paste in a blender, add 125 ml (½ cup) of stock and blend to a paste.

2 Heat the oil over low heat and cook the paste for 3–5 minutes, stirring constantly to prevent it burning or sticking. Add the remaining stock, bring to the boil, then reduce the heat and simmer for 15 minutes, or until reduced slightly.

3 Add the coconut milk, lime leaves, lime juice, fish sauce and palm sugar, and simmer for 5 minutes. Add the prawns and simmer for 2 minutes, or until they are pink and cooked through. Do not boil or cover.

4 Soak the vermicelli in boiling water for 5 minutes, or until soft. Drain and divide among serving bowls with most of the sprouts. Ladle hot soup over the noodles and garnish each bowl with tofu, mint, coriander and the remaining bean sprouts. Serve with lime wedges.

LOBSTER SOUP WITH ZUCCHINI AND AVOCADO

SERVES 4

50 g (1¾ oz) butter

1 garlic clove, crushed

2 French shallots, finely chopped

1 onion, chopped

1 zucchini (courgette), diced

2½ tablespoons dry white wine

400 ml (14 fl oz) fish stock

250 g (9 oz) raw lobster meat, chopped

250 ml (9 fl oz/1 cup) thick (double/ heavy) cream

1 avocado, diced

1 tablespoon chopped coriander (cilantro) leaves

1 tablespoon chopped parsley

lemon juice, to serve

1 **Melt the butter** in a large saucepan. Add the garlic, chopped shallots, onion and zucchini. Cook over medium heat for 8–10 minutes, or until the vegetables are just soft.

2 **Splash in the wine** and bring to the boil, keeping on the boil for 3 minutes.

3 **Pour in the stock** and bring to the boil again. Reduce the heat to low, add the chunks of lobster and simmer for 3–4 minutes, or until the lobster meat is opaque and tinged pink. Gently stir in the cream and season with salt and freshly ground black pepper.

4 **To serve,** ladle the soup into four bowls and stir a little of the avocado, coriander and parsley into each one. Squeeze a little lemon juice over the soup before serving.

Note: You can substitute the lobster with crayfish or prawns (shrimp).

MEXICAN SOUP WITH SALSA

SERVES 4

60 ml (2 fl oz/¼ cup) olive oil

1 large onion, chopped

1 large celery stalk, chopped

3 garlic cloves, crushed

2 small thin red chillies, seeded and finely chopped

200 ml (7 fl oz) fish stock

800 g (1 lb 12 oz) tinned chopped tomatoes

2 bay leaves

1 teaspoon dried oregano

1 teaspoon caster (superfine) sugar

2 large cobs of corn, kernels removed

500 g (1 lb 2 oz) halibut fillets, skinned

2 tablespoons chopped coriander (cilantro) leaves

juice of 2 limes

12 prawns (shrimp), peeled and deveined, tails intact

8 scallops, cleaned

12 clams, cleaned

125 g (4 fl oz/½ cup) thick (double/ heavy) cream

SALSA

½ small avocado

1 tablespoon coriander (cilantro) leaves

finely grated zest and juice of 1 lime

½ small red onion, finely chopped

1 **Heat the oil** in a large saucepan. Add the onion and celery and cook over medium heat for 10 minutes, stirring now and then. Add the garlic and chilli to the pan and cook 1 minute, stirring. Add the fish stock and tomatoes and break up the tomatoes in the pan using a wooden spoon. Stir in the bay leaves, oregano and sugar and bring to the boil. Allow to bubble for 2 minutes, then reduce the heat to low and gently simmer for 10 minutes. Cool for 5 minutes, remove the bay leaves, then tip the tomato mixture into a food processor or blender and process until fairly smooth. Alternatively, push the mixture through a coarse sieve or mouli by hand.

2 **Return the tomato sauce** to the saucepan and season with salt. Add corn kernels and bring back to the boil. Reduce the heat to a simmer to cook for 3 minutes, or until the kernels are just tender.

3 **Cut the fish** into large chunks. Stir the coriander and the lime juice into the sauce, add the fish to the pan, then simmer gently for a minute. Add the prawns and scallops and scatter the clams on the top. Cover with a lid and cook gently for a further 2–3 minutes, or until the seafood is opaque and cooked through, the prawns have turned pink and the clams have steamed open. Discard any clams that are unopened.

4 **While the fish is poaching,** make the salsa. Chop the avocado into small cubes and mix with the coriander, the lime zest and juice, and red onion and season with salt and pepper. Before serving, stir the cream into the soup, ladle into deep bowls and top with salsa. Serve with sourdough.

Note: You can substitute the fish with swordfish or snapper.

CHUNKY FISH SOUP WITH BACON AND DUMPLINGS

SERVES 6

2 tablespoons olive oil

1 onion, chopped

1 small red capsicum (pepper), chopped

1 small zucchini (courgette), diced

150 g (5½ oz) smoked bacon, chopped

1 garlic clove, crushed

2 tablespoons paprika

400 g (14 oz) tin chopped tomatoes

400 g (14 oz) tin chickpeas

450 g (1 lb) skinless fish fillet (any firm white fish), cut into large pieces

2 tablespoons chopped flat-leaf (Italian) parsley, to serve

DUMPLINGS

75 g (2½ oz) self-raising flour

1 egg, lightly beaten

1½ tablespoons milk

2 teaspoons finely chopped marjoram

1 **Heat the oil** in a large saucepan, then add the onion. Cook over low heat for 8–10 minutes, or until softened. Add the capsicum, zucchini, bacon and garlic and cook over medium heat for 5 minutes, stirring now and then.

2 **Meanwhile,** make the dumpling mixture by combining the flour, egg, milk and marjoram together in a bowl with a wooden spoon.

3 **Add the paprika,** tomato, chickpeas and 800 ml (28 fl oz) water to the vegetables in the saucepan. Bring the liquid to the boil, then reduce the heat to low and simmer gently for 10 minutes, or until thickened slightly.

4 **Using two tablespoons** to help you form the dumplings, add six rounds of dumpling mixture to the soup (this should use up all the mixture). Poach for 2 minutes, then slide the pieces of fish into the liquid. Poach for a further 2–3 minutes, or until the fish is cooked. The dumplings and fish should be ready simultaneously. Season to taste, sprinkle with parsley, then serve.

SALADS

GRILLED SALMON WITH FENNEL AND ORANGE SALAD

SERVES 4

FENNEL AND ORANGE SALAD
1 fennel bulb, with fronds
2 oranges, peeled and segmented
12 pitted black olives
1 tablespoon snipped chives
3 tablespoons virgin olive oil
2 tablespoons lemon juice
1 teaspoon Dijon mustard
½ teaspoon caster (superfine) sugar

500 g (1 lb 2 oz) piece salmon fillet
1 tablespoon virgin olive oil
200 g (7 oz) baby English spinach leaves

1   To prepare the salad, trim the fronds from the fennel bulb and finely chop up enough fronds to fill a tablespoon. Remove the stalks from the fennel and cut a 5 mm (¼ inch) thick slice off the base of the bulb. Cut the bulb in half, then finely slice and toss in a large bowl with the chopped fronds, orange segments, olives and chives. In a separate bowl, whisk the oil with the lemon juice, mustard and sugar. Season to taste, pour over the fennel mixture and toss gently to coat.

2   Heat the grill (broiler) to medium. Remove the bones and skin from the salmon and cut the flesh into 1 cm (½ inch) thick slices. Put the salmon in a shallow dish, add the oil, and season with salt and pepper. Toss gently to coat, then place on a lightly greased grill tray. Grill for 1–2 minutes, or until just cooked through.

3   Divide the spinach leaves among four large serving plates, top with the fennel and orange salad and arrange the salmon over the spinach. Serve warm.

Note: Fennel bulbs are easily sliced using the slicing disc of a food processor.

SMOKED TROUT AND KIPFLER POTATO SALAD

SERVES 4

6 hickory woodchips

2 rainbow trout

1 tablespoon oil

750 g (1 lb 10 oz) even-sized kipfler (fingerling) potatoes, peeled

3 baby fennel bulbs, cut into quarters, then into eighths

2 tablespoons olive oil

40 g (1½ oz/2 cups) watercress sprigs

dill and caper dressing

125 g (4½ oz/½ cup) whole-egg mayonnaise

2 garlic cloves, crushed

1 tablespoon chopped dill

1 tablespoon baby capers, drained, rinsed and chopped

1 tablespoon lemon juice

1 **Soak the woodchips** in water overnight, or for a minimum of 30 minutes.

2 **Preheat a kettle** or covered barbecue to low indirect heat. Allow the coals to burn down to ash, then add three hickory woodchips to each pile of coals. When the chips begin to smoke, brush the trout with the oil, place in the middle of the barbecue, then lower the lid and cook for 10–15 minutes, or until the trout are cooked through. (If you don't have a coal barbecue, use the method outlined on page 322 for smoking racks of lamb.)

3 **Meanwhile,** preheat the barbecue chargrill plate to medium–high and bring a saucepan of water to the boil on the stovetop. Add the potatoes to the pan and cook for 5 minutes, or until almost tender. Drain well and allow to cool slightly. Combine the dill and caper dressing ingredients in a small bowl and refrigerate until needed.

4 **Cut the potatoes** into 1.5 cm (⅝ inch) slices on the diagonal. Place in a bowl with the fennel and olive oil, season with salt and freshly ground black pepper and toss to coat. Chargrill the potatoes for 5 minutes on each side, or until golden and cooked. Remove from the heat and place in a serving bowl. Chargrill the fennel for 2–3 minutes on each side, or until golden, then add to the potato slices.

5 **Remove the skin** from the smoked trout and gently pull the flesh away from the bones. Flake the flesh into pieces and add to the potato with the watercress and fennel. Pour on the dressing and serve immediately.

BARBECUED SQUID WITH SALSA VERDE

SERVES 4

4 cleaned squid tubes

3 tablespoons olive oil

3 garlic cloves, crushed

150 g (5½ oz) mixed lettuce leaves

250 g (9 oz/1 punnet) cherry tomatoes, halved

SALSA VERDE

2 large handfuls flat-leaf (Italian) parsley

2 tablespoons chopped dill

2 tablespoons extra virgin olive oil

2 tablespoons olive oil

1 tablespoon Dijon mustard

2 garlic cloves, crushed

1 tablespoon red wine vinegar

1 tablespoon baby capers, rinsed and drained

4 anchovy fillets, drained

1 **Open out the squid tubes** by cutting through one side so you have one large piece, the inside facing upwards. Pat dry with paper towels. Using a sharp knife, and being careful not to cut all the way through, score the flesh on the diagonal in a series of lines about 5 mm (¼ inch) apart, then do the same in the opposite direction to form a crisscross pattern. Cut the squid into 4 cm (1¼ inch) pieces and put in a non-metallic bowl. Combine the oil and garlic and pour over the squid, tossing to coat well. Cover and marinate in the refrigerator for 30 minutes.

2 **Put all the salsa verde** ingredients in a food processor and blend until just combined. Set aside until ready to use.

3 **Preheat a barbecue flat plate** to high. Drain the squid and cook for 1–2 minutes, or until curled up and just cooked through.

4 **Put the squid** in a bowl with the salsa verde and toss until well coated. Arrange the lettuce and tomatoes on four serving plates, top with the squid, then season and serve at once.

STEAMED PRAWNS WITH GREEN MANGO SALAD

SERVES 4

DRESSING

2 teaspoons lime juice

1 tablespoon fish sauce

1 garlic clove, crushed

½ teaspoon rice vinegar

½ teaspoon soft brown sugar

2 tablespoons fresh coconut juice or

2 teaspoons coconut milk mixed with 1½ tablespoons water (see Note)

12 large raw prawns (shrimp), peeled and deveined, tails removed

1 large red chilli, seeded and thinly shredded

3 red Asian shallots, finely sliced

1 large green mango, peeled and shredded (see Note)

1 large handful coriander (cilantro) leaves

2 kaffir lime leaves, shredded

1 **To make the dressing,** combine the lime juice, fish sauce, garlic, vinegar, sugar and coconut juice in a bowl.

2 **Line a bamboo steamer** with baking paper and punch with holes. Arrange the prawns in a single layer in the steamer. Sit the steamer over a wok of simmering water and steam, covered, for 3–4 minutes, or until the prawns turn opaque.

3 **Combine the chilli,** shallots, mango, coriander and lime leaves in a bowl. Add the prawns to the salad, drizzle on the dressing and toss gently to coat. Serve at once or at room temperature.

Note: Fresh coconut juice is not the same as coconut milk. The juice is the liquid found inside the coconut, whereas coconut milk and cream are extracted from the coconut flesh. Coconut juice and green mangoes can be found in Asian food stores and larger general supermarkets.

CUMIN, TUNA AND LEMONGRASS SALAD

SERVES 4

2 teaspoons minced red chilli

2 garlic cloves, crushed

2 teaspoons ground cumin

1 teaspoon ground turmeric

2 tablespoons lime juice

300 g (10½ oz) tuna steaks, about 2 cm (¾ inch) thick

125 ml (4 fl oz/½ cup) peanut oil

8 new potatoes, peeled and halved

2 tablespoons cumin seeds, lightly roasted

2 red Asian shallots, halved and finely sliced

2 stems lemongrass, white part only, trimmed and finely chopped

2 garlic cloves, finely chopped

2 small red chillies, deseeded and finely chopped

2 kaffir lime leaves, finely shredded

3 tablespoons lime juice, extra

1 Combine the minced chilli, garlic, cumin, turmeric and lime juice in a small bowl. Place the tuna steaks in a shallow glass or ceramic dish and season with salt and pepper. Spread the marinade over the tuna, coating both sides well. Cover with plastic wrap and refrigerate for 2–4 hours.

2 Heat the oil in a large frying pan and cook the tuna over a high heat for 3 minutes on each side. Remove the tuna from the pan and set aside to cool slightly, reserving the cooking oil. Cook the potatoes in boiling water until tender.

3 Combine the cumin seeds, shallots, lemongrass, garlic, chillies and lime leaves in a large salad bowl. Flake the tuna into small pieces and add to the lemongrass mixture. Add the lime juice, strained reserved warm oil and hot potato halves and toss to combine. Season to taste.

SASHIMI SALAD WITH WASABI DRESSING

SERVES 4–6

600 g (1 lb 5 oz) sashimi-grade tuna or salmon

½ small daikon radish or red radish

4 handfuls mizuna or baby rocket (arugula) leaves

1 Lebanese (short) cucumber

WASABI DRESSING

2 teaspoons wasabi paste

1 garlic clove, crushed

½ teaspoon finely grated fresh ginger

¼ teaspoon caster (superfine) sugar

1 tablespoon lime juice

1 tablespoon mirin

1½ tablespoons rice vinegar

2 tablespoons vegetable oil

¼ teaspoon toasted sesame oil

soy sauce, to season

1 **Cut the fish** into very thin, even slices with a sharp knife. Overlap the fish slices, circling inwards, to form a thin cover over a large serving plate. Cover and refrigerate until ready to use.

2 **Peel the daikon,** then using the fine tooth blade on a Japanese mandolin, or a very sharp knife and a steady hand, finely julienne the daikon then squeeze out any excess moisture. Chop the mizuna into 3 cm (1¼ inch) lengths. If using baby rocket, keep whole. Very finely slice the cucumber lengthways to form long thin ribbons (a vegetable peeler is good for this). Refrigerate all the salad ingredients until chilled.

3 **To make the dressing,** whisk together the wasabi, garlic, ginger, sugar, lime juice, mirin, rice vinegar, vegetable and sesame oils. Season to taste with a few drops of soy sauce and a small pinch of salt and set aside.

4 **When ready to serve,** combine the daikon, mizuna and cucumber, then toss together with the dressing. Place the salad mixture in the centre of the plate, drizzle any excess dressing over the fish and serve immediately.

STEAMED PRAWN AND NOODLE SALAD

SERVES 4

2 tablespoons Chinese rice wine

pinch of sugar

1 tablespoon fish sauce

20 raw king prawns (shrimp), peeled and deveined, tails removed

90 g (3¼ oz/1 bunch) coriander (cilantro)

80 g (2¾ oz/1 bunch) mint

200 g (7 oz) dried rice vermicelli

4 tablespoons lime juice

4 tablespoons peanut or vegetable oil

1 teaspoon sesame oil

5 cm (2 inch) piece fresh ginger, thinly sliced on the diagonal

1 **Combine the rice wine,** sugar and fish sauce in a bowl. Add the prawns and toss them through the mixture. Cover and leave to marinate for 10 minutes.

2 **Divide the bunch of coriander** in two and set aside one half. Finely chop half of the remaining coriander and pick the whole leaves from the stems that are left (reserve these for the garnish). Repeat with the bunch of mint.

3 **Cook the vermicelli** according to the packet instructions. Drain well and put in a large bowl. Add the lime juice, peanut oil, sesame oil and the chopped coriander and mint. Season with salt and black pepper and toss well.

4 **Put a shallow heatproof bowl** inside a bamboo steamer and line it with ginger slices and the reserved half bunches of coriander and mint. Sit the prawns and any liquid on the herbs and steam over a wok of simmering water for about 5 minutes, or until the prawns are pink and cooked through. Carefully remove the bowl from the steamer.

5 **Divide the vermicelli** among four serving plates. Top with the prawns and the cooking juices and garnish with the whole coriander and mint leaves.

CHARGRILLED PRAWN SALAD WITH SAFFRON AÏOLI

SERVES 4

AÏOLI

3 teaspoons lemon juice

small pinch of saffron threads

2 egg yolks

3 garlic cloves, minced

1 teaspoon dijon mustard

230 ml (8 fl oz) olive oil

¼–½ teaspoon cayenne pepper, to taste

250 g (9 oz/1½ cups) shelled broad (fava) beans

16 asparagus spears, sliced in half on the diagonal

300 g (10½ oz) watercress

1 avocado

250 g (9 oz/2 cups) yellow teardrop tomatoes, halved

20 raw prawns (shrimp), peeled and deveined

1 tablespoon olive oil

1 teaspoon lemon juice

sea salt, to taste

1 **To make the aïoli,** put the lemon juice and saffron in a small bowl and set aside for 30 minutes. Transfer to a mini processor and add the egg yolks, garlic and mustard. Whizz for 8–10 seconds, or until smooth, scraping down the side of the bowl if necessary. With the motor running, gradually add the olive oil. Season with salt and cayenne pepper, to taste.

2 **Bring a saucepan** of water to the boil and add the broad beans and a large pinch of salt. Simmer over medium heat for 4 minutes. Scoop out the beans with a slotted spoon and rinse under cold water. Add the asparagus to the water and blanch for 1 minute, or until just tender. Drain, rinse under cold water and transfer to a shallow salad bowl.

3 **Peel off and discard** the broad bean skins. Add the broad beans to the asparagus. Pick the top leaves from the watercress, leaving some of their stalks on. Halve the avocado, cut the flesh into chunks and add to the salad, along with the watercress and tomatoes.

4 **Preheat the barbecue plate** or chargrill pan to medium–high. Toss the prawns in the combined oil and lemon juice, to coat and grill for 45 seconds on each side, or until just cooked through.

5 **Add the prawns** to the salad, season with sea salt and freshly ground black pepper and toss lightly. Serve the salad accompanied by the aïoli.

SALMON AND PASTA SALAD

SERVES 4

500 g (1 lb 2 oz) salmon steaks

2 tablespoons lemon juice

300 g (10½ oz) penne

3 tablespoons red wine vinegar

1 tablespoon dijon mustard

125 ml (4 fl oz/½ cup) olive oil

80 g (2¾ oz/½ cup) pine nuts, toasted

200 g (7 oz/heaped ¾ cup) ricotta cheese, crumbled

1 handful basil, roughly chopped

4 tablespoons roughly chopped flat-leaf (Italian) parsley

35 g (1¼ oz/⅓ cup) coarsely grated parmesan cheese

80 g (2¾ oz/1¾ cups) baby rocket (arugula)

200 g (7 oz) cherry tomatoes, halved

1 Line a steamer with baking paper and punch with holes. Place the salmon steaks on top and cover with a lid. Sit the steamer over a saucepan or wok of boiling water and steam for 5 minutes, or until just cooked (they should still be a little pink in the centre). Remove from the steamer. When the steaks are cool enough to handle, remove the skin and bones and break the flesh into chunks. Drizzle with lemon juice and season with salt and freshly ground black pepper.

2 Cook the penne according to the packet instructions, then drain and leave to cool.

3 To make a quick dressing, put the vinegar and mustard in a small jar and shake well. Add the oil and shake until combined.

4 Put the salmon, penne, pine nuts, ricotta, basil, parsley, parmesan, rocket and tomatoes in a large bowl, drizzle with the dressing and toss gently to combine.

OCTOPUS, ARTICHOKE AND FETA SALAD

SERVES 4

800 g (1 lb 12 oz) baby octopus, cleaned (see Note)

3 teaspoons oregano, finely chopped

2 garlic cloves, finely chopped

1 long red chilli, seeded and finely chopped

3 teaspoons lime zest

4 tablespoons lime juice

3 tablespoons extra virgin olive oil

100 g (3½ oz/¾ cup) baby green beans, trimmed

125 g (4½ oz/5 cups) baby rocket (arugula)

1 handful mint, leaves torn if large

250 g (9 oz) marinated artichoke hearts, drained and halved

120 g (4¼ oz) marinated feta cheese, roughly crumbled

1½ tablespoons baby salted capers, rinsed and squeezed dry

1 In a non-metallic bowl, combine the octopus, oregano, garlic, chilli, lime zest, 2 tablespoons of lime juice and 2 tablespoons of oil. Season well, then cover with plastic wrap and marinate in the refrigerator for 30 minutes.

2 Line a steamer with baking paper and punch with holes. Place the octopus and beans on top in a single layer and cover with a lid. Sit the steamer over a saucepan or wok of boiling water and steam for 5 minutes, or until cooked through. Allow to cool for 5 minutes, reserving the cooking juices.

3 Scatter the rocket and mint leaves on a serving dish, then add the artichoke, feta, capers, beans and octopus. Combine the remaining lime juice, oil and 1 tablespoon of the cooking juices. Drizzle over the salad, toss gently, then season and serve.

Note: Ask your fishmonger to clean the octopus for you.

MARINATED PRAWNS WITH MANGO CHILLI SALSA

SERVES 4–6

LEMON DILL MARINADE
4 tablespoons lemon juice

4 tablespoons olive oil

1 teaspoon sea salt

3 tablespoons chopped dill

1 kg (2 lb 4 oz) raw prawns (shrimp), peeled and deveined, tails intact

150 g (5½ oz/1 bunch) rocket (arugula)

MANGO CHILLI SALSA
450 g (1 lb/1½ cups) diced fresh or tinned mango

1 red onion, finely diced

1 small red chilli, seeded and finely chopped

1 tablespoon grated lemon zest

1 **Put the lemon dill** marinade ingredients in a large non-metallic bowl and mix well. Add the prawns, toss well, then cover and refrigerate for 1 hour.

2 **Preheat the barbecue flat plate** to moderately high. Just before you're ready to eat, put the mango chilli salsa ingredients in a bowl, mix well and set aside.

3 **Drain the prawns** from the marinade and cook them on the hotplate for about 2–4 minutes, turning once, or until they have changed colour but are still soft and fleshy to touch. Take them off the heat straight away and let them cool slightly.

4 **Arrange a bed of rocket** on individual serving plates. Add a generous scoop of salsa, then the prawns. Season to taste and serve at once.

FRESH SEAFOOD SALAD WITH SPICY LIME DRESSING

SERVES 4

DRESSING

4 thin slices of young galangal, chopped

1 long green chilli, deseeded and finely sliced

1 garlic clove, crushed

2 tablespoons lime juice

1 tablespoon rice vinegar

1 tablespoon fish sauce

1½ tablespoons mirin

1 teaspoon sugar

3 tablespoons vegetable oil

SEAFOOD SALAD

250 g (9 oz) piece sashimi-grade salmon fillet

250 g (9 oz) squid tubes, scored and cut into 5 cm (2 inch) pieces

8 scallops, shelled

8 raw king prawns (shrimp), peeled and deveined, tails intact

1 large avocado, chopped into dice

150 g (5½ oz) snow peas (mangetout), trimmed and cut lengthways into thin strips

60 g (2¼ oz) bean sprouts, trimmed

½ small red onion, finely sliced

150 g (5½ oz) baby Asian greens

1 **In a mortar and pestle,** pound the galangal until broken down into smaller pieces. Add the green chilli and garlic and pound until a paste forms. Remove and put into a small bowl with the remaining dressing ingredients and whisk until combined.

2 **Heat 2 tablespoons of oil** in a large frying pan over medium–high heat. Sear the salmon fillet for 1 minute on each side. Remove, cover and set aside.

3 **In the remaining oil,** cook the squid tubes, scallops and prawns separately until cooked. Remove and cover. Drizzle 2 tablespoons of the dressing over the seafood.

4 **Combine the vegetables** with the seafood. Break large pieces of the salmon from the fillet, allowing 2–3 pieces per person. Divide the salmon and remaining seafood over the salad ingredients. Drizzle with the remaining dressing.

BARBECUE PRAWNS WITH WATERMELON AND FETA

SERVES 4

12 raw prawns (shrimp), peeled and
    deveined, tails intact

1 tablespoon olive oil

2 teaspoons sumac (see Note)

1 kg (2 lb 4 oz) seedless watermelon,
    peeled and cut into 2 cm (¾ inch)
    pieces

½ small red onion, finely sliced

30 g (1 oz/¼ cup) pitted black olives

150 g (5½ oz) feta cheese

1 tablespoon extra virgin olive oil

1 tablespoon lemon juice

2 tablespoons chopped mint

1 **Mix the prawns** with the olive oil and 1 teaspoon of sumac and allow to marinate for 15 minutes.

2 **Heat a barbecue flat plate** or grill plate to medium–high and cook the prawns in batches for 3–5 minutes, or until golden and cooked through. Remove from heat.

3 **Divide the watermelon,** onion, and olives among four large plates. Crumble the feta over the salad in large pieces.

Combine the oil, lemon juice, remaining sumac and mint. Season well and drizzle over the salad. Top with the prawns and serve immediately.

Note: Sumac is a purplish coloured spice with a lemony taste.

SQUID AND CHICKPEA SALAD

SERVES 4–6

4 cleaned squid tubes (see Note)

100 g (3½ oz/½ cup) couscous

4 tablespoons extra virgin olive oil

400 g (14 oz) tin chickpeas, drained and rinsed

3 spring onions (scallions), finely sliced

2 tomatoes, seeded and cut into 5 mm (¼ inch) dice

90 g (3¼ oz/½ cup) green olives, pitted and halved

1 large handful parsley, chopped

2 garlic cloves, crushed

3 tablespoons lemon juice

1 small red chilli, seeded and finely sliced

1 Cut the squid into 5 mm (¼ inch) strips, arrange the strips in a steamer and cover with a lid. Sit the steamer over a saucepan or wok of boiling water and steam for 4 minutes, or until just cooked.

2 Put the couscous in a small bowl with 125 ml (4 fl oz/ ½ cup) of cold water. Leave for 5 minutes then add 1 teaspoon of the olive oil and work it through the couscous with your fingers.

3 Line a small steamer with a clean, damp cloth — a tea towel (dish towel) is fine — tip the couscous onto the tea towel, then cover and steam over simmering water for 20 minutes. Break up any clumps gently with a fork two or three times during the cooking time.

4 Tip the couscous into a bowl, add 1 teaspoon of olive oil and use a fork to gently separate the grains. Leave to cool.

5 Combine the squid, couscous, chickpeas, spring onion, tomato, olives, parsley, garlic, lemon juice, chilli and remaining oil in a large bowl, season and mix well.

Note: You can buy cleaned squid tubes from your fishmonger.

CUTTLEFISH AND FENNEL SALAD

SERVES 4

750 g (1 lb 10 oz) cuttlefish or squid,
  cleaned and cut into thin strips

1 small fennel bulb, finely sliced,
  reserving the fronds

½ red onion, finely sliced

80 g (2¾ oz/3 cups) rocket (arugula)

DRESSING

2 tablespoons lime juice

1 tablespoon sherry vinegar

1 garlic clove, crushed

¼ teaspoon chilli flakes

3 tablespoons extra virgin olive oil

1 tablespoon wholegrain mustard

1 **Place the cuttlefish** on a plate in a steamer and cover with a lid. Sit the steamer over a saucepan or wok of boiling water and steam for about 3 minutes, or until just cooked. Cool, then place in a bowl with the fennel, onion and 2 tablespoons of the finely chopped fennel fronds.

2 **Mix all the dressing ingredients** together in a bowl or a screw-top jar and pour over the salad. Toss gently and season to taste.

3 **Arrange the rocket** leaves on a serving plate and top with the salad.

CAESAR SALAD WITH SARDINES

SERVES 4

DRESSING

1 egg

2 garlic cloves

2 tablespoons lemon juice

½ teaspoon Worcestershire sauce

3–4 anchovy fillets

125 ml (4 fl oz/½ cup) olive oil

100 g (3 oz/1 cup) dry breadcrumbs

65 g (2/3 cup) grated Parmesan cheese

2 tablespoons chopped fresh parsley

2 eggs, lightly beaten

80 ml (3 fl oz/1/3 cup) milk

16 sardines, scaled and butterflied

oil, for deep-frying

12 small pappadoms

1 baby cos lettuce, leaves separated

8 slices of prosciutto, cooked until crisp

50 g (2 oz/½ cup) shaved Parmesan cheese

1 **To make the dressing,** put the egg in a food processor, add the garlic, lemon juice, Worcestershire sauce and anchovies and process to combine. With the motor running, add the oil in a thin, steady stream until the dressing has thickened slightly. Set aside until you're ready to serve.

2 **Put the breadcrumbs,** grated Parmesan and parsley in a bowl and mix well. Put the beaten eggs and milk in another bowl and whisk well. Dip the sardines into the egg wash, then into the crumb mixture, and put on a paper-lined baking tray. Refrigerate for an hour.

3 **Heat the oil** in a deep-fat fryer or heavy-based frying pan until 180°C (350°F), or until a small cube of white bread dropped into the oil browns in 15 seconds. Deep-fry the pappadoms until crisp, then drain on paper towels. Deep-fry the sardines in batches until crisp and golden.

4 **Arrange the lettuce** on a plate, top with prosciutto, sardines, pappadoms and Parmesan, then drizzle with the dressing.

Note: You can substitute the sardines with small herring, mackerel or prawns.

SMOKED SALMON AND ROCKET SALAD

SERVES 4

DRESSING

2 tablespoons extra virgin olive oil

1 tablespoon balsamic vinegar

150 g (1 bunch) rocket (arugula) leaves

1 avocado

250 g (9 oz) smoked salmon slices

325 g (11½ oz) marinated goat's cheese, drained and crumbled

2 tablespoons roasted hazelnuts, roughly chopped

1 For the dressing, thoroughly whisk together the oil and vinegar in a bowl. Season to taste.

2 Trim the long stems from the rocket. Rinse the leaves, pat dry and gently toss in a bowl with the dressing.

3 Cut the avocado into wedges. Put about three wedges on each serving plate with the salmon and rocket. Scatter the cheese and nuts over the top and season with freshly ground black pepper.

Note: You can use smoked trout in place of smoked salmon.

LEMON-SCENTED SCALLOPS WITH FENNEL

SERVES 4

1 lemon, sliced

400 g (14 oz) large scallops, roe removed

1 tablespoon grated lemon zest

1 baby fennel bulb, finely sliced

3 radishes, finely sliced

60 g (2¼ oz/2 cups) watercress, trimmed

1½ tablespoons roughly snipped chives

80 g (2¾ oz/½ cup) ligurian olives

2 tablespoons mayonnaise

2 teaspoons dijon mustard

1½ teaspoons lemon juice

1 Line a steamer with baking paper and punch with holes, then top with a layer of lemon slices. Place the scallops in a single layer on top, sprinkle with the lemon zest and cover with a lid. Sit the steamer over a saucepan or wok of simmering water and steam for 4 minutes, or until just cooked through. Allow to cool.

2 Combine the fennel, radish, watercress, chives and olives in a bowl.

3 Make a dressing by whisking together the mayonnaise, mustard and lemon juice. Season to taste.

4 Divide the fennel salad among four plates, top with the scallops and drizzle the dressing over the top.

SMOKED TUNA AND WHITE BEAN SALAD

SERVES 4

100 g (2 handfuls) rocket (arugula)

1 small red capsicum (pepper), cut into matchsticks

1 small red onion, chopped

310 g (11 oz) tin cannellini beans, drained and rinsed

125 g (4 oz) cherry tomatoes, cut into halves

2 tablespoons capers, rinsed and squeezed dry

2 x 125 g (4½ oz) tins smoked tuna slices in oil, drained

BASIL DRESSING

1 tablespoon lemon juice

1 tablespoon white wine

60 ml (2 oz/¼ cup) extra virgin olive oil

1 garlic clove, crushed

2 tablespoons chopped basil

½ teaspoon sugar

1   **Trim any long stems** from the rocket, rinse, pat dry and divide among four serving plates.

2   **Lightly toss the capsicum** in a large bowl with the onion, beans, tomatoes and capers. Spoon some onto each plate, over the rocket, then scatter tuna over each.

3   **For the dressing,** thoroughly whisk all the ingredients in a bowl with 1 tablespoon of water, ¼ teaspoon of salt and freshly ground black pepper, to taste. Drizzle over the salad and serve with bread.

PEPPERY PRAWN NOODLE SALAD

SERVES 4

DRESSING

1 teaspoon sichuan pepper

2 spring onions (scallions), finely chopped

1 tablespoon grated fresh ginger

1 tablespoon soy sauce

1 tablespoon fish sauce

¼ teaspoon sesame oil

1 tablespoon lime juice

1 teaspoon soft brown sugar

100 g (3½ oz) mung bean vermicelli

700 g (1 lb 9 oz) cooked king prawns (shrimp), peeled and deveined, tails intact

½ telegraph (long) cucumber, sliced in half, seeds removed and sliced on diagonal

2 large vine-ripened tomatoes, sliced into wedges

140 g (5 oz/1⅔ cups) bean sprouts, trimmed

1 large handful mint

1 handful coriander (cilantro) leaves

3 spring onions (scallions), sliced

20 g (¾ oz/¼ cup) crisp fried shallots

1 **In a small bowl,** combine the dressing ingredients. Soften the vermicelli according to packet instructions and cut with a pair of scissors.

2 **Toss the prawns,** cucumber, tomatoes, bean sprouts, mint, coriander, spring onions and noodles together with the dressing. Divide among four plates, top with the fried shallots and serve immediately.

NIÇOISE SALAD WITH FRESH TUNA

SERVES 4

DRESSING

6 anchovy fillets, drained

2 tablespoons red wine vinegar

1 large garlic clove, crushed

125 ml (4 fl oz/½ cup) olive oil

750 g (1 lb 10 oz) new potatoes

1 cos (romaine) lettuce, shredded

1 Lebanese (short) cucumber, cut into
    1 cm (½ inch) slices on the diagonal

½ red capsicum (pepper), thinly sliced

200 g (7 oz) green beans, trimmed
and blanched

2 tomatoes, each cut into 8 wedges

1 small red onion, cut into thin wedges

200 g (7 oz) black olives

2 large handfuls basil leaves, torn

olive oil, for brushing

600 g (1 lb 5 oz) fresh tuna steaks

3 hard-boiled eggs, quartered

1 **To make the dressing,** put the anchovies, vinegar and garlic in a food processor and blend until the anchovies are finely chopped. With the motor running, slowly add the oil and blend until combined.

2 **Bring a large saucepan** of water to the boil. Add the potatoes and cook for about 10 minutes, or until tender. Drain well, allow to cool a little, then peel and cut into 1 cm (½ inch) slices. Put the potato in a large bowl with the lettuce, cucumber, capsicum, beans, tomato, onion, olives and basil. Pour the dressing over. Gently toss to combine.

3 **Preheat a barbecue grill plate** or chargrill pan to high. Brush the hotplate with oil and cook the tuna for 2 minutes on each side — it should still be a little pink in the middle. Slice the tuna into 2 cm (¾ inch) cubes.

4 **Arrange the salad** on four serving plates and top with the tuna and egg quarters. Season with salt and freshly ground black pepper and serve immediately.

REDFISH IN CORN HUSKS WITH ASPARAGUS SALAD

SERVES 6

SALAD

1 red capsicum (pepper)

2 tablespoons virgin olive oil

1 small garlic clove, crushed

1 tablespoon lemon juice

1 tablespoon chopped basil

1 tablespoon pine nuts

100 g (4 oz/½ cup) small black olives

6 small red mullet or other small fish, scaled and gutted

12 sprigs of lemon thyme

1 lemon, sliced

2 garlic cloves, sliced

12 large corn husks

olive oil, for drizzling

2 bunches of fresh asparagus, trimmed

lemon wedges, for serving

1 **To make the salad,** cut the capsicum into large pieces. Put skin-side up under a hot griller (broiler) until the skin blackens and blisters. Alternatively, hold over the coals or gas flame of a barbecue. Cool in a plastic bag, then peel off the skin. Finely dice the flesh.

2 **Combine the olive oil,** garlic, lemon juice and basil in a small bowl and whisk together. Add the capsicum, pine nuts and olives.

3 **Wash the fish** and pat dry inside and out with paper towels. Fill each fish cavity with thyme, lemon and garlic, then place each in a corn husk. Drizzle with oil and sprinkle with pepper, then top each fish with another husk. Tie each end of the husks with string to enclose.

4 **Place the fish** on coals or on a barbecue and cook, turning once, for 6–8 minutes, or until the fish is cooked and flakes easily when tested with a fork. A few minutes after you've started cooking the fish, brush the asparagus with oil and cook, turning occasionally, on the barbecue for 3–4 minutes, or until tender. Pour the dressing over the asparagus and serve with the fish and salad.

MAINS

DEEP-FRIED FISH WITH CHILLI JAM

SERVES 4

CHILLI JAM

1 tablespoon oil

1 red onion, finely chopped

4 garlic cloves, crushed

2 tablespoons finely chopped coriander (cilantro) roots and stems

6 long red chillies, seeded and finely chopped

1½ tablespoons hoisin sauce

1½ tablespoons fish sauce

95 g (3¼ oz/½ cup) soft brown sugar

125 g (4½ oz/1 cup) self-raising flour

1 teaspoon salt

125 ml (4 fl oz/½ cup) chilled sparkling mineral water

vegetable oil, for deep-frying

4 white fish fillets (such as perch, barramundi or snapper)

coriander (cilantro) leaves, to serve

1 **To make the chilli jam,** heat a wok over high heat, add the oil and swirl to coat. Cook the onion for 2–3 minutes. Add the garlic, coriander and chilli and cook for 1 minute. Stir in the hoisin sauce, fish sauce, sugar and 100 ml (3½ fl oz) of water and cook for 8 minutes, or until reduced.

2 **Make a batter** by sifting the flour and salt into a bowl. Add the mineral water and 4 tablespoons of cold water and whisk until smooth.

3 **Fill a wok** one-third full of oil and heat to 180°C (350°F), or until a cube of bread dropped in the oil browns in 15 seconds. Dip one piece of fish at a time into the batter and deep-fry in the oil for 2–3 minutes, or until the fish is golden and cooked. Drain on crumpled paper towels. Repeat with the remaining fish and batter. Serve topped with the chilli jam and garnish with coriander.

SESAME-COATED SALMON WITH CORIANDER RELISH

SERVES 4

CORIANDER RELISH

2 large handfuls coriander (cilantro) leaves

2 tablespoons chopped coriander (cilantro) stems

2 garlic cloves, crushed

3 spring onions (scallions), chopped

1 teaspoon ground cumin, dry-fried

1 tablespoon desiccated coconut

2 teaspoons lime juice

3 tablespoons coconut milk

3 teaspoons fish sauce

vegetable oil, for deep-frying

4 large garlic cloves, very finely sliced

4 salmon fillets, skin and all bones removed

2 egg whites, beaten until frothy

155 g (5½ oz/1 cup) white sesame seeds

1 **To make the relish,** put all the ingredients in a food processor and process until combined. Spoon into a small bowl.

2 **Fill a wok** one-third full of oil and heat to 180°C (350°F), or until a cube of bread dropped in the oil browns in 15 seconds. Deep-fry the garlic for 30 seconds, or until lightly golden and crisp. Drain on crumpled paper towels.

3 **Coat the salmon fillets** in the egg white, letting any excess drip off, then coat in the sesame seeds. Deep-fry the salmon in batches for 2 minutes, or until cooked but still pink in the centre. Drain on crumpled paper towels. Sprinkle the garlic chips over the top and serve with the coriander relish.

STIR-FRIED SQUID FLOWERS WITH CAPSICUM

SERVES 4

400 g (14 oz) squid tubes

3 tablespoons oil

2 tablespoons salted fermented black beans, mashed

1 small onion, cut into small cubes

1 small green capsicum (pepper), cut into small cubes

3–4 small slices fresh ginger

1 spring onion (scallion), cut into short lengths

1 small red chilli, chopped

1 tablespoon Chinese rice wine

½ teaspoon roasted sesame oil

1   **Open up the squid tubes** and scrub off any soft jelly-like substance, then score the inside of the flesh with a fine criss-cross pattern, making sure you do not cut all the way through. Cut the squid into 3 x 5 cm (1¼ x 2 inch) pieces.

2   **Blanch the squid** in a saucepan of boiling water for 25–30 seconds — each piece will curl up and the criss-cross pattern will open out, hence the name 'squid flower'. Remove and refresh in cold water, then drain and dry well.

3   **Heat a wok** over high heat, add the oil and heat until very hot. Stir-fry the black beans, onion, capsicum, ginger, spring onion and chilli for about 1 minute. Add the squid and rice wine, mix well and stir for 1 minute. Sprinkle with the sesame oil and serve immediately.

SHANGHAI-STYLE FIVE-WILLOW FISH

SERVES 4

3–4 dried Chinese mushrooms

650 g (1 lb 7 oz) whole fish, scaled, gutted, with head and tail intact

1 teaspoon salt

oil, for deep-frying, plus 2 tablespoons extra

1 tablespoon finely sliced fresh ginger

2 tablespoons finely sliced spring onions (scallions)

½ small carrot, finely sliced

½ small green capsicum (pepper), finely sliced

½ celery stalk, finely sliced

2 red chillies, seeded and finely sliced

2 tablespoons light soy sauce

3 tablespoons sugar

3 tablespoons rice vinegar

1 tablespoon Chinese rice wine

125 ml (4 fl oz/½ cup) chicken stock

1 tablespoon cornflour (cornstarch)

½ teaspoon roasted sesame oil

1 **Soak the mushrooms** in hot water for 20 minutes, then drain and squeeze out any excess water. Remove and discard the stems. Finely shred the caps.

2 **Clean and dry the fish** well. Diagonally score both sides of the fish, cutting through as far as the bone at intervals of about 2 cm (¾ inch) — this will help the heat penetrate and allow the fish to cook. Rub the fish with the salt, inside and out.

3 **Fill a wok** one-third full of oil and heat to 190°C (375°F), or until a cube of bread dropped in the oil browns in about 10 seconds. Using tongs, carefully lower the fish into the oil, belly-side-down, curling it to fit the curves of the wok. Cook for 6–8 minutes, spooning oil over the top of the fish. Remove from the wok and drain on crumpled paper towels. Place fish on a long serving dish. Keep warm in a low oven.

4 **Remove the oil** and wipe out the wok. Heat the wok over high heat, add the extra oil and heat until very hot. Stir-fry the mushrooms, ginger, spring onion, carrot, capsicum, celery and chilli for 1½ minutes. Add the soy sauce, sugar, rice vinegar, rice wine and stock, and bring to the boil. Mix the cornflour with enough water to make a paste. Add the cornflour paste to the sauce and simmer until the sauce thickens. Sprinkle with the sesame oil and blend well. Spoon the sauce over the fish and serve immediately.

Note: This is a variation of the classic 'sweet and sour fish' recipe from the Yangtze River delta, a region that's characterized by its delicate fish and rice dishes and use of tender vegetables. 'Five-willow' refers to the five types of vegetables that have been finely sliced for the sauce.

CRAB WITH SPICES, CORIANDER AND CHILLI

SERVES 4

4 small or 2 large live crabs

2 garlic cloves, very finely chopped

2 teaspoons finely grated fresh ginger

¼ teaspoon ground cumin

¼ teaspoon ground coriander

¼ teaspoon ground turmeric

¼ teaspoon cayenne pepper

1 tablespoon tamarind purée

1 teaspoon sugar

2 small red chillies, seeded and finely chopped

125 ml (4 fl oz/½ cup) oil

2 tablespoons chopped coriander (cilantro) leaves

1 Put the crabs in the freezer for 1 hour to immobilize them. Using a large heavy-bladed knife or cleaver, cut the crabs in half (or quarters if you are using the large ones) and scrape out the spongey grey gills, then twist off and crack the claws. Turn the body over and pull off the apron pieces. Rinse well under cold running water and pat dry.

2 Arrange the crabs in a single layer in a large steamer and cover with a lid. Sit the steamer over a wok or saucepan of boiling water and steam for 4–5 minutes, or until half cooked. Remove from the heat.

3 Mix together the garlic, ginger, cumin, ground coriander, turmeric, cayenne pepper, tamarind, sugar, chilli, half the oil and a generous pinch of salt.

4 Heat the remaining oil in a large deep frying pan over medium heat. When the oil is hot, add the spice mixture and stir for 30 seconds.

5 Add the crabs and cook, stirring, for 2 minutes, making sure the spice mix is rubbed into the cut edges of the crab.

6 Add 125 ml (4 fl oz/½ cup) of water, then cover and steam the crabs for a further 5–6 minutes, or until cooked. The crabs will turn pink or red when they are ready and the flesh will turn opaque.

7 To serve, drizzle a little of the liquid from the pan over the crabs and scatter with the coriander leaves. Serve with crab crackers, picks, finger bowls and bread.

Note: This recipe also works well with large prawns (shrimp).

THAI MUSSELS WITH NOODLES

SERVES 4

2 kg (4 lb 8 oz) mussels

235 g (8½ oz/4 small bundles) glass noodles

boiling water, for soaking

2 garlic cloves, crushed

2 spring onions (scallions), finely chopped

125 ml (4 fl oz/½ cup) fish stock

2 tablespoons Thai red curry paste

170 ml (6 fl oz/⅔ cup) coconut cream

juice of 2 limes

2 tablespoons fish sauce

1 handful coriander (cilantro) leaves

1 **Rinse the mussels** in cold water and pull out the hairy beards. Discard any broken mussels, or open ones that don't close when tapped on a bench.

2 **Soak the glass noodles** in boiling water for 8–10 minutes. Drain and, using a pair of scissors, cut them into shorter lengths.

3 **Put the mussels,** garlic and spring onion in a large steamer and cover with a lid. Sit the steamer over a wok or saucepan of boiling water and steam for 4–5 minutes, or until they are all open. Throw away any mussels that don't open.

4 **Pour the fish stock** into a large saucepan, add the curry paste and coconut cream and stir together. Bring the mixture to the boil, then add the lime juice and fish sauce. Put the mussels back in the pan, cook for 1 minute, then stir in the coriander.

5 **To serve,** divide the noodles among bowls and ladle the mussels and broth over the top.

THAI GREEN FISH CURRY

SERVES 4

CURRY PASTE

2 teaspoons shrimp paste

2 long green chillies, seeded

8 bird's eye chillies, seeded

4 garlic cloves

4 red Asian shallots, peeled

4 coriander (cilantro) roots

3 cm (1¼ inch) piece galangal, chopped

1 stem lemongrass, chopped

2 kaffir lime leaves, finely chopped

1 teaspoon ground cumin

1 teaspoon ground coriander

5 white peppercorns

1 tablespoon peanut oil

250 ml (9 fl oz/1 cup) thick coconut cream

400 ml (14 fl oz) tin coconut milk

6 kaffir lime leaves, crushed

100 g (3½ oz) snake beans, cut into 3 cm (1 inch) lengths

230 g (8½ oz) tin bamboo shoots, drained

200 g (7 oz) broccoli, cut into small florets

500 g (1 lb 2 oz) firm white fish fillets, cut into 3 cm (1¼ inch) pieces

1 handful Thai basil leaves

1 To make the paste, wrap the shrimp paste in foil and toast in a hot wok for 1 minute on each side. Remove the foil and put the shrimp paste in a food processor with the chillies, garlic, shallots, coriander roots, galangal, lemongrass, lime leaves, cumin, coriander, peppercorns, oil and 1 tablespoon of water. Blend until smooth.

2 Put the coconut cream in a wok and cook over high heat for 5 minutes, or until the oil starts to separate from the cream. Add 3 tablespoons of the curry paste and cook for 2 minutes, or until aromatic. Add the coconut milk, lime leaves, snake beans, bamboo shoots and broccoli and cook for 3–4 minutes. Add the fish and cook for 2–3 minutes, or until cooked through. Stir in the basil and serve with steamed rice. Freeze any leftover paste for next time.

MARINATED STEAMED SALMON

SERVES 4

10 cm (4 inch) piece lemongrass

5 cm (2 inch) piece fresh ginger, finely grated

2 tablespoons sweet chilli sauce

1 small red chilli, seeded and finely chopped

1 tablespoon fish sauce

2 tablespoons lime juice

1 tablespoon vegetable oil

4 tablespoons chopped coriander (cilantro) leaves

4 x 180 g (6 oz) salmon fillets

2 spring onions (scallions), finely chopped

1 **Remove the outer layers** of the lemongrass and finely chop the rest. Combine in a bowl with ginger, sweet chilli sauce, chilli, fish sauce, lime juice, oil and 2 tablespoons of the coriander. Mix well using a fork.

2 **Put the salmon** in a shallow non-metallic dish and pour the marinade over the top. Cover and refrigerate for 1 hour. Remove from marinade, allowing any excess to drip off.

3 **Line a bamboo steamer** with baking paper and punch with holes. Arrange the salmon fillets on top in a single layer. Sit the steamer over a wok of simmering water, making sure the bottom of the steamer doesn't touch the water, and steam, covered, for 10–12 minutes, depending on how well you want the salmon cooked. Combine the remaining coriander with the spring onion and scatter over the salmon before serving.

MUSSELS IN CHUNKY TOMATO SAUCE

SERVES 6

1.5 kg (3 lb 5 oz) black mussels

1 tablespoon olive oil

1 large onion, diced

4 garlic cloves, finely chopped

800 g (1 lb 12 oz) tinned chopped
   tomatoes

3 tablespoons tomato paste
   (concentrated purée)

30 g (1 oz/¼ cup) pitted black olives

1 tablespoon capers, rinsed and
   squeezed dry

125 ml (4 fl oz/½ cup) fish stock

3 tablespoons chopped flat-leaf (Italian)
   parsley

1 Scrub the mussels with a stiff brush and pull out the hairy beards. Discard any damaged mussels, or any that don't close when tapped on the bench.

2 In a large saucepan, heat the olive oil and cook the onion and garlic over medium heat for 1–2 minutes, or until softened. Add the tomato, tomato paste, olives, capers and fish stock. Bring to the boil, then reduce the heat and simmer, stirring occasionally, for 20 minutes, or until the sauce is thick.

3 Stir in the mussels and cover the saucepan. Shake or toss the mussels occasionally and cook for 4–5 minutes, or until the mussels begin to open. Remove the pan from the heat and discard any mussels that haven't opened in the cooking time. Add the parsley, toss gently and serve.

PRAWNS IN BANANA LEAVES

SERVES 4

2.5 cm (1 inch) piece ginger, grated

2 small red chillies, seeded and finely chopped

4 spring onions (scallions), finely chopped

2 lemongrass stems, white part only, finely chopped

2 teaspoons grated palm sugar (jaggery) or soft brown sugar

1 tablespoon fish sauce

2 tablespoons lime juice

1 tablespoon sesame seeds, toasted

2 tablespoons chopped coriander (cilantro) leaves

1 kg (2 lb 4 oz) raw prawns (shrimp), peeled and deveined

8 small banana leaves (see Note)

boiling water, for soaking

1 **Put the ginger,** chilli, spring onion and lemongrass in a food processor and pulse in short bursts until a paste forms (alternatively, you can do this in a mortar and pestle). Transfer the paste to a bowl, then stir in the sugar, fish sauce, lime juice, sesame seeds and coriander and mix well. Add the prawns and toss to coat. Cover and marinate in the refrigerator for 2 hours.

2 **Meanwhile,** put the banana leaves in a large heatproof bowl, cover with boiling water and leave them to soak for 3 minutes, or until softened. Drain and pat dry. Cut the banana leaves into 18 cm (7 inch) squares.

3 **Divide the prawn mixture** into eight, and place one portion on each square of banana leaf. Fold the leaf to enclose the mixture, and then secure the parcels with a wooden skewer. Put the parcels in a steamer and cover with a lid. Sit the steamer over a wok or saucepan of boiling water and steam for 8–10 minutes, or until the filling is cooked.

Note: Banana leaves are used throughout Asia to wrap foods for steaming or baking. They keep the food moist and impart a mild flavour. Buy them from Asian food stores if you don't have access to fresh leaves.

FISH IN SPICED NUT SAUCE

SERVES 4

NUT SAUCE

16 almonds

2 cm (¾ inch) piece fresh ginger,
    roughly chopped

2–3 red bird's eye chillies, seeded

5 red Asian shallots, roughly chopped

2 garlic cloves

1 large roma (plum) tomato or
    2 medium ones, roughly chopped

2 teaspoons fish sauce

2 teaspoons palm sugar (jaggery) or soft
    brown sugar

2 spring onions (scallions), sliced

4 x 180 g (6 oz) white fish fillets (such
    as perch, barramundi or snapper)

banana leaves, blanched, to wrap
    (available from Asian supermarkets)

lemon or lime wedges, to serve

1 **To make the nut sauce,** heat a frying pan over high heat. Add the almonds and dry-fry for 4–5 minutes. Cool. Put the almonds, ginger, chillies, shallots, garlic, tomato and ½ teaspoon of salt in a small food processor or blender and process until smooth. Stir in the fish sauce, sugar and half the spring onion.

2 **Spread the paste** over the fish fillets. Cut out four pieces of banana leaf large enough to enclose the fish. Sit the fish in the middle of the leaves, fold in the sides and roll over to tightly enclose in the leaves.

3 **Put the fish parcels** in a bamboo steamer. Sit the steamer over a wok of simmering water and steam, covered, for 7–8 minutes, or until the fish flakes when tested. Remove from the parcels and garnish with the remaining spring onion. Serve with lemon or lime wedges and steamed rice.

STEAMED SNAPPER WITH GINGER AND SHALLOTS

SERVES 4

6 spring onions (scallions), sliced on the diagonal

2 small (400 g/14 oz each) whole snapper, cleaned and scaled

2 teaspoons salt

2 teaspoons sesame oil

3 tablespoons light soy sauce

3 tablespoons finely sliced fresh ginger

60 g (2¼ oz) fresh shiitake mushrooms, sliced

2 tablespoons peanut oil

1½ tablespoons Chinese rice wine

coriander (cilantro) sprigs (optional), to serve

1   Lightly oil two plates large enough to hold each fish and sit them in two layers of a bamboo steamer. Take half the spring onions and divide between the two plates. Pat the fish dry with paper towels, then lay the fish on top of the spring onion. Combine the salt, sesame oil and 2 tablespoons of soy sauce and rub the mixture over each fish. Scatter the ginger and mushrooms over the fish, putting some in each cavity.

2   Sit the steamers over a wok of simmering water and steam, covered, for 30 minutes, or until the fish is just cooked through. Swap the steamers over halfway through cooking. Remove the plates from the steamer.

3   Heat the peanut oil in a small saucepan over medium heat until it starts to smoke — the oil must be hot enough to crisp the skin of the fish, otherwise it will taste oily. Drizzle the rice wine and remaining soy sauce evenly over the fish, then scatter with the remaining spring onion. Gently pour the hot oil over the whole length of the fish (take care as it will sizzle and splatter). Serve immediately, garnished with the coriander sprigs.

GREEK-STYLE CALAMARI

SERVES 4–6

STUFFING

1 tablespoon olive oil

2 spring onions (scallions), chopped

280 g (9 oz/1½ cups) cold, cooked rice (see Note)

60 g (2¼ oz) pine nuts

75 g (3 oz/½ cup) currants

2 tablespoons chopped parsley

2 teaspoons finely grated lemon zest

1 egg, lightly beaten

1 kg (2 lb 4 oz) squid (calamari) tubes, washed and patted dry

SAUCE

4 large ripe tomatoes

1 tablespoon olive oil

1 onion, finely chopped

1 garlic clove, crushed

60 ml (2 oz/¼ cup) good-quality red wine

1 tablespoon chopped fresh oregano

1 **Preheat the oven** to 160°C (315°F/Gas 2–3).

2 **For the stuffing,** mix the oil, spring onion, rice, pine nuts, currants, parsley and lemon zest in a bowl. Season well with salt and freshly ground black pepper. Add enough egg to moisten all the ingredients. Three-quarters fill each squid tube with the stuffing. Secure the ends with toothpicks. Put in a single layer in a casserole dish.

3 **For the sauce,** score a cross in the base of each tomato, put in a bowl of boiling water for 30 seconds, then plunge into cold water and peel the skin away from the cross. Chop the flesh.

4 **Heat the oil** in a pan. Add the onion and garlic and cook over low heat for 2 minutes, or until the onion is soft. Add the tomato, wine and oregano and bring to the boil. Reduce the heat, cover and cook over low heat for 10 minutes.

5 **Pour the hot sauce** over the squid, cover and bake for 20 minutes, or until the squid is tender. Remove the toothpicks before cutting into thick slices for serving. Spoon the sauce over the calamari just before serving.

Note: You will need to cook 100 g (½ cup) rice for this recipe.

BLUE EYE COD WITH GARLIC AND PARSLEY MAYONNAISE

SERVES 4

MAYONNAISE

3 garlic cloves, chopped

2 tablespoons chopped flat-leaf (Italian) parsley

2 egg yolks

1 teaspoon finely grated lime zest

1 teaspoon dijon mustard

125 ml (4 fl oz/½ cup) grapeseed oil

2–3 teaspoons lime juice, to taste

20 g (¾ oz) butter

2 teaspoons grapeseed oil

4 skinless blue eye cod fillets or other large-fleshed white fish fillets

1   To make the mayonnaise, put the garlic and parsley in a mini processor and whizz in 3-second bursts for 30 seconds, or until finely chopped. Add the egg yolks, lime zest and mustard. With the motor running, gradually add the oil and whizz for 25–40 seconds, or until thick and creamy. Add the lime juice, to taste, and season well with salt and freshly ground black pepper. Whizz briefly to combine.

2   Heat the butter and oil in a large non-stick frying pan over medium heat. Add the fish fillets and cook for 3–4 minutes each side, or until cooked through. Drain on paper towels.

3   Transfer the fish to warm serving plates and top with some of the mayonnaise.

Note: Creamy polenta and a tomato salad make ideal accompaniments. Store any leftover mayonnaise in an airtight jar in the refrigerator for up to 1 week.

SEARED TUNA WITH MILD CHILLI AND ORANGE DRESSING

SERVES 4

DRESSING

zest and juice of 1 orange

1 tablespoon finely chopped rosemary

1 handful mint

1 small handful flat-leaf (Italian) parsley

1 bird's eye chilli, seeded and finely chopped

1 tablespoon red wine vinegar

2 tablespoons walnut oil

80 ml (2½ fl oz/⅓ cup) olive oil

400 g (14 oz) tin chickpeas, drained

1 small red onion, thinly sliced

1 large handful baby English spinach

4 tuna steaks, 2.5 cm (1 inch) thick

1 tablespoon olive oil

sea salt, to taste

1 **To make the dressing,** put the orange zest, rosemary, mint, parsley and chilli in a small processor fitted with the metal blade. Whizz for 30–40 seconds, or until finely chopped. With the motor running, add the orange juice, vinegar and oils and whizz for 20 seconds.

2 **Put the chickpeas,** onion and spinach in a bowl, add 2 teaspoons of the dressing and toss to combine.

3 **Brush the tuna steaks** with the olive oil and season with sea salt and freshly ground black pepper. Preheat the barbecue plate or chargrill to high. Add the tuna and cook until done to your liking.

4 **Serve the tuna** on a bed of chickpea salad, drizzled with the remaining dressing.

OCEAN TROUT FILLETS WITH CORIANDER AND LIME CREAM

SERVES 4

CREAM

1 large handful coriander (cilantro) leaves

2 tablespoons chopped coriander (cilantro) stems

grated zest of 1 lime

1 tablespoon lime juice

150 g (5½ oz/⅔ cup) crème fraîche or sour cream

4 x 185 g (6½ oz) ocean trout fillets, skin on

olive oil, for brushing

sea salt, to taste

snow pea sprouts, trimmed, to serve

lime wedges, to serve

1 **To make the cream,** put the coriander leaves and stems, lime zest, lime juice and crème fraîche or sour cream in a blender or small processor fitted with the metal blade. Whizz for 35–50 seconds, or until the mixture is creamy.

2 **Preheat the barbecue** or chargrill pan to high. Brush both sides of the ocean trout fillets with a little olive oil and rub the skin well with sea salt and freshly ground black pepper. Reduce the heat to medium and add the trout fillets, skin side down. Fry for 3 minutes each side for medium, or until done to your liking. Remove from the heat and rest in a warm place for 2 minutes.

3 **Arrange the trout fillets** on a bed of snow pea sprouts on four serving plates, skin side down, and spoon a dollop of coriander and lime cream on top. Serve with lime wedges.

Note: The cream can be made in advance and chilled in an airtight container for up to 45 minutes before use. It will change texture if left any longer.

WHOLE FISH WITH GARLIC AND CORIANDER MARINADE

SERVES 4

MARINADE

4 large garlic cloves, chopped

4 coriander (cilantro) roots including
    10 cm (4 inches) stems, chopped

1 teaspoon white peppercorns

1 tablespoon oyster sauce

1 tablespoon light soy sauce

1 teaspoon fish sauce

1.25 kg (2 lb 12 oz) whole snapper,
    scaled and cleaned, or 2 x 750 g
    (1 lb 10 oz) snapper

1–2 banana leaves

vegetable oil spray

1 small handful chopped coriander
    (cilantro) leaves and stems

1 **To make the marinade,** put the garlic, coriander roots and stems and peppercorns in a mini processor and whizz for 10–15 seconds, or until chopped. Add the oyster sauce, soy sauce and fish sauce and whizz for 20 seconds, or until smooth.

2 **Pat the fish dry** with paper towels. Slash the flesh on each side two to three times. Layer pieces of banana leaves evenly over a large sheet of foil and lightly spray with oil. Put the fish on the banana leaves.

3 **Spoon the marinade** evenly over the fish, including in the cavity. Put the chopped coriander leaves and stems in the cavity. Enclose the fish in the banana leaves and foil and seal. Refrigerate for 2 hours.

4 **Preheat the barbecue** to medium. Cook the wrapped fish, turning occasionally, for 25–30 minutes. Open the parcel and check for doneness. If the flesh is not opaque all the way through, return to the heat until cooked.

5 **Carefully unwrap the fish** and transfer to a serving platter. Serve immediately.

Note: Steamed jasmine rice and lime wedges are ideal accompaniments to this dish.

TUNA STEAKS WITH GREEN OLIVE PASTE

SERVES 4

OLIVE PASTE

2 slices white bread, crusts removed

1 handful flat-leaf (Italian) parsley

2 teaspoons grated lemon zest

2 teaspoons lemon juice

1 garlic clove, chopped

80 g (2¾ oz/⅔ cup) pitted green olives

1 tablespoon olive oil

4 x 185 g (6½ oz) tuna steaks

2 tablespoons lemon juice

2 tablespoons white wine

90 g (3 oz) unsalted butter

1 Preheat the oven to 200°C (400°F/Gas 6).

2 **To make the olive paste,** put the bread and parsley in a small processor fitted with the metal blade. Whizz for 30 seconds, or until the mixture forms breadcrumbs. Add the lemon zest, lemon juice, garlic and olives. Whizz for 10 seconds, or until the mixture comes together. With the motor running, slowly add the olive oil to form a smooth paste. Season well with salt and freshly ground black pepper.

3 **Put the tuna steaks** in an ovenproof dish. Spread some olive paste evenly over the tuna. Pour the lemon juice and wine around the tuna. Bake for 12–15 minutes, or until done to your liking. The tuna should still be pink in the centre.

4 **Meanwhile,** melt the butter in a saucepan over medium heat and cook until the butter turns a nut brown colour. Transfer the tuna to serving plates and drizzle with the melted butter.

Note: The tuna is delicious served on a bed of potato mash. Store any leftover olive paste in an airtight container in the refrigerator for up to a week.

NORTH AFRICAN SPICED FISH PARCELS

SERVES 4

2 large all-purpose potatoes, washed, unpeeled

olive oil, for brushing

4 x 220 g (8 oz) thick skinless blue eye cod fillets or snapper fillets

2 vine-ripened tomatoes, thinly sliced lengthways

PASTE

1 small onion, roughly chopped

2 garlic cloves

1 dried red chilli, crumbled

2 teaspoons cumin seeds

1 teaspoon sweet paprika

1 handful flat-leaf (Italian) parsley

1 handful coriander (cilantro) leaves

4 anchovy fillets

grated zest and juice of 1 lemon

80 ml (2½ fl oz/⅓ cup) extra virgin olive oil

salad greens, to serve

1 Parboil the potatoes in boiling salted water for 10 minutes. Drain and set aside to cool for 15 minutes. Cut each potato lengthways into six slices.

2 Preheat the oven to 200°C (400°F/Gas 6). Line a baking sheet with baking paper. Cut four 30 cm (12 inch) squares of baking paper and foil. Put the baking paper squares on top of the foil squares and brush the centre of each with oil. Set aside.

3 To make the paste, put the onion, garlic, chilli, cumin seeds and paprika in a mini processor. Whizz for 1 minute, or until a coarse paste forms. Add the parsley, coriander, anchovies, lemon zest, lemon juice and oil and whizz for 40 seconds, or until evenly chopped.

4 Brush the paste all over the fish fillets, coating them thoroughly.

5 Divide the potato and tomato slices among the prepared foil and paper squares, making an even layer on each. Season with salt and freshly ground black pepper and top with the fish fillets. Pull one side of each square over the top of the fish to meet the opposite side. Fold the edges over tightly to seal the parcels. Put the parcels on the prepared baking sheet and bake for 25 minutes.

6 Break the parcels open with a sharp knife. Using a large spatula, transfer the fish and vegetables to plates and serve immediately, accompanied with salad greens.

ISLAND BAKED SNAPPER

SERVES 4

PASTE

235 g (8½ oz/4 cups) shredded coconut

1 green papaya

grated zest of 2 limes

125 ml (4 fl oz/½ cup) lime juice

400 ml (14 fl oz) coconut milk

sea salt, to taste

2 kg (4 lb 8 oz) whole snapper

1 **To make the paste,** preheat the oven to 180°C (350°F/ Gas 4). Divide the shredded coconut between two shallow baking tins lined with baking paper and toast for 10–15 minutes, or until golden.

2 **Halve the papaya** lengthways, scrape out the seeds and peel the flesh. Roughly chop the papaya and put in a small processor fitted with the metal blade. Whizz for 15 seconds, or until finely chopped. Transfer to a large bowl.

3 **Add the toasted coconut,** lime zest, lime juice and coconut milk to the processor and whizz for 15–20 seconds, or until semi-smooth. Add to the papaya and season with sea salt.

4 **Lightly rinse** the cavity of the snapper and dry the fish with paper towels. Put the fish in a roasting tin lined with baking paper. Smother both sides of the fish with the paste. Cover with foil and refrigerate for 1 hour.

5 **Preheat the oven** to 190°C (375°F/Gas 5). Remove the foil and bake the fish for 40–45 minutes, or until cooked through. Serve whole on a platter, accompanied by lime wedges.

VIETNAMESE-STYLE SEAFOOD CURRY

SERVES 4

CURRY PASTE

1 tablespoon coriander seeds

2 teaspoons cumin seeds

1 teaspoon dried chilli flakes

2 teaspoons shrimp paste

4 garlic cloves, chopped

2 stems lemongrass, white part only, chopped

2 cm (¾ inch) piece fresh turmeric, chopped

5 spring onions (scallions), chopped

3 cm (1¼ inch) piece fresh ginger, chopped

2 tablespoons vegetable oil

400 ml (14 fl oz) tin coconut cream

125 ml (4 fl oz/½ cup) chicken stock

3 cm (1 inch) piece galangal, sliced

600 g (1 lb 5 oz) pumpkin, peeled, seeded and cut into 2.5 cm (1 inch) pieces

300 g (10½ oz) firm white fish fillets, cut into 2.5 cm (1 inch) pieces

16 raw prawns (shrimp), peeled and deveined, tails intact

12 scallops without roe

1½ tablespoons fish sauce

1 small handful Vietnamese mint, torn

1   To make the curry paste, put the coriander and cumin seeds and chilli in a hot wok and dry-fry over high heat for 30 seconds, or until aromatic. Transfer to a spice grinder and grind to a powder. Wrap the shrimp paste in foil and heat in a hot wok for 1 minute on each side. Add to the spices in the grinder with the garlic, lemongrass, turmeric, spring onion, ginger, oil and 1 tablespoon of water and grind to a smooth paste.

2   Heat a wok over high heat, add the paste and cook for 1 minute, or until aromatic. Add the coconut cream, stock, galangal and pumpkin and cook over high heat for 4–5 minutes, or until the pumpkin is tender.

3   Add the fish, prawns and scallops and cook for 2–3 minutes, or until cooked through. Stir in the fish sauce and mint and serve with rice.

MEE SIAM

SERVES 4

120 g (4½ oz) dried rice vermicelli

1 tablespoon shrimp paste

4 red Asian shallots, peeled

3 garlic cloves, crushed

8 long dried red chillies, soaked in boiling water for 10 minutes, seeds removed

2 teaspoons dried shrimp, soaked in boiling water for 10 minutes, drained

3 tablespoons peanut oil

12 raw king prawns (shrimp), peeled and deveined, tails intact

90 g (3 oz/1 cup) bean sprouts, tails trimmed

BROTH

85 g (3 oz/⅓ cup) yellow bean sauce (taucheo)

2½ tablespoons tamarind purée

1 teaspoon caster (superfine) sugar

1 onion, halved, finely sliced horizontally into half rings

8 fried square tofu puffs, halved diagonally, to serve

2 hard-boiled eggs, quartered, to serve

2 limes, cut into wedges, to serve

4 garlic chives, snipped, to serve

crisp fried shallots, to serve

1 **Put the noodles** in a bowl, cover with boiling water and soak for 5 minutes. Drain well and set aside.

2 **Wrap the shrimp paste** in foil and toast in a hot wok for 1 minute on each side. Remove the foil and put the paste in a food processor with the shallots, garlic, dried chillies and dried shrimp. Blend to form a paste, adding water if necessary.

3 **Heat a wok** over high heat, add 1 tablespoon of oil and swirl to coat. Stir-fry the prawns for 2–3 minutes, or until pink and cooked through. Remove.

4 **Add another tablespoon of oil** and stir-fry the paste for 1 minute, or until fragrant. Remove half the paste and set aside. Add 250 ml (9 fl oz/1 cup) of water to the wok with salt, to taste. Stir to combine and bring to a simmer.

5 **Add the noodles** and cook for about 3–4 minutes, then add the bean sprouts and cook for 1 minute, or until all the liquid evaporates.

6 **Meanwhile,** to make the broth, combine the ingredients in a saucepan with 1 litre (35 fl oz/4 cups) of water and bring to the boil. Add the reserved spice paste, stirring well, then simmer for 5 minutes.

7 **To serve,** divide the noodle mixture among four deep serving bowls. Ladle on the broth, then top each bowl with prawns, tofu puffs, boiled eggs and lime wedges. Garnish with the chives and crisp fried shallots and serve immediately.

SALMON, RICOTTA AND RED ONION FRITTATA

SERVES 4

2 red onions, cut into 5 mm (¼ inch) thick slices

2 tablespoons olive oil

150 g (5½ oz) baby English spinach leaves

8 eggs

2 spring onions (scallions), finely chopped

200 g (7 oz) sliced smoked salmon

100 g (3½ oz) ricotta cheese

light sour cream, to serve

1 Heat the grill (broiler) to high. Spread the onion on a lightly greased oven tray, lightly brush with some of the oil and grill for 2–3 minutes, or until nicely browned. Gently flip the onions over, brush with a little more oil if needed and grill for another 2–3 minutes. Remove from the tray and set aside. Turn the grill down to medium.

2 While the onion is grilling, bring a saucepan of water to the boil. Add the spinach and blanch for 30 seconds, then drain and refresh in cold water. Squeeze out any liquid and roughly chop the leaves.

3 Beat the eggs in a bowl, season with salt and pepper, then stir in the spinach and grilled onion.

4 Heat the remaining oil in a 21 cm (8 inch) non-stick frying pan, add the spring onion and sauté over medium heat for about 1 minute, or until soft.

5 Stir the spring onion through the egg mixture, then pour the mixture back into the pan. Roll the smoked salmon slices into small rosettes and arrange them around the frittata. Spoon small dollops of ricotta in between the salmon rosettes.

6 Cook the frittata on the stovetop over medium heat for about 10 minutes, moving the pan around over the heat to ensure even cooking. When the frittata is cooked halfway through, put the pan under the grill and cook for 5–10 minutes, or until the top is golden brown and the frittata is cooked through. If the frittata starts to brown too quickly, cover it with a sheet of foil.

7 To serve, slide or invert the frittata onto a plate, slice it into wedges, sprinkle with cracked black pepper and a dollop of sour cream.

TUNA WITH BAKED EGGPLANT

SERVES 4

MARINADE

pinch of saffron threads

3 tablespoons olive oil

2 tablespoons lemon juice

1 tablespoon pomegranate molasses,
    optional (see Note)

1 small onion, grated

1 large garlic clove, crushed

1 tablespoon dried oregano

1 teaspoon cumin seeds

pinch of kirmizi biber (see Note),
    or crushed dried chilli

1 teaspoon nigella seeds (see Note),
    or ½ teaspoon cracked black pepper

1 teaspoon coriander seeds, crushed

4 x 200 g (7 oz) tuna fillets (see Note)

1 small eggplant (aubergine), chopped

90 g (3 oz/½ cup) toasted pine nuts

120 g (4 oz) lamb's lettuce (corn salad)

2 tablespoons roughly torn mint leaves

3 tablespoons olive oil

1 tablespoon red wine vinegar

16 small pitted black olives

1 **To make the marinade,** soak the saffron in 1 tablespoon of hot water in a small bowl. Leave to infuse for 10 minutes. Add a generous pinch of salt, then all the remaining marinade ingredients. Mix well. Put the tuna in a single layer in a shallow non-metallic dish and pour the marinade all over, ensuring the fish is thoroughly coated. Cover and refrigerate for 2 hours.

2 **Heat the grill** (broiler) to high. Lift the tuna fillets out of the marinade, reserving the marinade, and sit them on a large baking tray with the eggplant chunks. Brush the eggplant and fish all over with the marinade. Grill for 5–8 minutes, or until the fish is cooked, turning the eggplant occasionally.

3 **Meanwhile,** toss the pine nuts, lettuce and mint in a bowl. Mix the oil with the vinegar, season to taste and toss through the salad. Divide the salad among four serving plates. Scatter with the olives and eggplant chunks and sit the tuna on top. Drizzle some of the cooking juices over the tuna and serve.

Note: Pomegranate molasses is a syrup with a sweet and sour taste. Kirmizi biber is a chilli pepper spice, and nigella seeds are small black seeds with an aromatic flavour. They are often sold in Middle Eastern grocery stores. This recipe is also delicious with perch, sea bass and swordfish.

FISH PIE

SERVES 4

POTATO TOPPING

500 g (1 lb 2 oz) floury potatoes
(eg. Idaho, King Edward), diced

60 ml (2 fl oz/¼ cup) milk or cream

1 egg, lightly beaten

30 g (1 oz) butter

60 g (2 oz) Cheddar cheese,
finely grated

800 g (1 lb 12 oz) skinless ling fillets (or
other white fish), cut into large chunks

375 ml (12 fl oz/1½ cups) milk

30 g (1 oz) butter

1 onion, finely chopped

1 garlic clove, crushed

2 tablespoons plain (all-purpose) flour

2 tablespoons lemon juice

2 teaspoons lemon zest

1 tablespoon chopped dill

1 Preheat the oven to 180°C (350°F/Gas 4).

2 To make the topping, steam the potatoes until tender. Mash, then push to one side of the pan, add the milk and heat gently. Beat the milk into the potato until it is fluffy, then season and stir in the egg and butter. Mix in half the Cheddar, then set aside and keep warm.

3 Put the fish in a frying pan and cover with the milk. Bring to the boil, then reduce the heat and simmer for 2 minutes, or until the fish is opaque and flaky. Drain, reserving the milk, and put the fish in a 1.5 litre (6 cup) ovenproof dish.

4 Melt the butter in a saucepan and cook the onion and garlic for 2 minutes. Stir in the flour and cook for 1 minute, or until pale and foaming. Remove from the heat and gradually stir in the reserved milk. Return to the heat and stir constantly until it boils and thickens. Reduce the heat and simmer for 2 minutes. Add the lemon juice, zest and dill, and season.

5 Mix with the fish. Spoon the topping over the fish and top with the remaining Cheddar. Bake for 35 minutes, or until golden.

Note: You can substitute the fish with snapper, monkfish, cod, haddock or flathead.

VINE-WRAPPED BLUE-EYE WITH DILL AND LEMON BUTTER

SERVES 4

8 fresh or preserved vine leaves

2 tablespoons chopped dill

60 g (2 oz) butter, softened

4 x 200 g (7 oz) blue-eye fillets (see Note)

1 tablespoon lemon juice

oil, for brushing

1 **If you are using fresh vine leaves,** bring a saucepan of water to the boil and blanch the leaves in batches for 30 seconds. Pat dry on crumpled paper towels. If you are using preserved vine leaves, simply rinse and dry them. Place 2 leaves on a work surface, slightly overlapping them. Repeat with the remaining leaves.

2 **Combine the dill** and butter in a small bowl and divide into four portions. Put each portion in the centre of each set of overlapping vine leaves. Rest a piece of fish on top of the butter and drizzle with the lemon juice. Season with salt and pepper. Wrap the fish in the vine leaves by bringing the edge closest to you over the fish, folding in the sides (if the leaves are wide enough) as you go, rolling up very firmly. Put the parcels on a plate, then cover and refrigerate for 30 minutes.

3 **Preheat a barbecue flat plate** to medium. Brush the hotplate with oil and grill the fish for 6–8 minutes, or until cooked through, turning once. Serve hot, with a Mediterranean-style salad.

Note: Any thick fish fillet can be used in this recipe if blue-eye is unavailable.

PEPPERED TUNA STEAKS WITH WASABI DRESSING

SERVES 4

4 x 250 g (9 oz) fresh tuna steaks

3 tablespoons soy sauce

3 tablespoons cracked black pepper

350 g (12 oz/2 bunches) young asparagus, trimmed and blanched

2 red onions, quartered

2 tablespoons olive oil

WASABI DRESSING

60 g (2 oz) thick plain yoghurt

3 tablespoons whole-egg mayonnaise

1 tablespoon lemon juice

2 teaspoons wasabi paste

1 tablespoon finely chopped dill

1 **Preheat a barbecue grill plate,** flat plate or chargrill pan to high. Toss the tuna steaks in the soy sauce, then coat liberally with the black pepper, pressing in well. Cover and refrigerate until ready to cook.

2 **In a small bowl,** combine the wasabi dressing ingredients and mix together well. Set aside until needed.

3 **Toss the asparagus** and onion in a bowl with the oil until coated all over. Grill them on the hotplate for about 5 minutes, or until the onion starts to brown. Remove from the heat and keep warm.

4 **Put the tuna** on the hotplate and cook for 3–5 minutes, turning once, or until the outside is browned and crisp — the tuna should still be a little pink in the middle. The exact cooking time will vary depending on the thickness of your tuna steaks. Slice the tuna into thick strips.

5 **Arrange the asparagus** and onion on four serving plates, top with the tuna slices and drizzle with a little wasabi dressing. Serve any remaining dressing on the side.

WHOLE OCEAN TROUT IN BANANA LEAVES

SERVES 8

2.5 kg (5 lb 8 oz) whole cleaned ocean trout

150 g (5½ oz/¾ cup) roughly chopped fresh ginger

3 stems lemongrass, white part only, sliced

18 kaffir lime leaves

125 ml (4 fl oz/½ cup) vegetable oil

2 teaspoons sea salt

2 lemons, sliced

2 large banana leaves, halved lengthways, centre vein removed

lemon or lime wedges, to serve

1 **Wash trout in cold water.** Pat dry inside and out with paper towels. Cut five deep slashes on each side of trout.

2 **Put the ginger,** lemongrass and 12 of the lime leaves in a food processor with the oil and salt. Blend to a paste. Rub the paste inside the cavity of the fish and all over the skin, rubbing well into the slits. Put the lemon slices and remaining lime leaves in the cavity of the trout, then sit the fish in a large dish, cover and refrigerate for several hours to allow the flavours to develop.

3 **Meanwhile,** preheat a kettle or covered barbecue to medium indirect heat. Bring a large saucepan of water to the boil. If the banana leaves are too large for the pan, cut them in half. Add the banana leaves in batches and simmer for 2 minutes, or until softened slightly. Remove and refresh in cold water.

4 **Put the banana leaves** on a work surface, overlapping them slightly. Now place the trout in the centre of the leaves, and carefully enclose the trout so it is fully covered by banana leaves. Tie into a parcel at frequent intervals with kitchen string. Rest trout on a cake rack and sit it on the barbecue grill. Lower lid and cook for 30 minutes. Carefully turn fish over using two large spatulas (you may need help). Grill 30 minutes, or until just cooked through.

5 **To serve,** put the trout on a large platter, carefully cut and remove the string. Cut along the centre of the banana leaves and open up, gently peel back the skin of the trout and carefully lift out large pieces of fish. Serve with fresh lemon or lime wedges, and a green salad and crusty bread.

Note: Banana leaves are available at speciality fruit and vegetable stores and Asian stores.

GOOD FORTUNE CLAMS

SERVES 4

120 g (4 oz) dried rice vermicelli

3 tablespoons vegetable oil

3 garlic cloves, crushed

2–3 teaspoons black bean chilli sauce (spicy black bean sauce)

1 kg (2 lb 4 oz) clams (vongole), soaked and cleaned

3 tablespoons Chinese rice wine

3 tablespoons chicken stock

2 teaspoons light soy sauce

3 tablespoons chopped coriander (cilantro) leaves

1 Soak the vermicelli in boiling water for 5 minutes. Drain well.

2 Heat a wok over medium–high heat, add the oil and swirl to coat. Stir-fry the garlic and black bean chilli sauce for about 30 seconds, or until fragrant. Add the clams, rice wine, stock and soy sauce. Increase the heat to high, then cover the wok with a lid and cook the clams, gently shaking occasionally, for 3–5 minutes, or until the clams have opened up.

3 Remove from the heat and discard any unopened clams. Add the vermicelli and toss gently. Scatter the chopped coriander over the top, toss gently and serve.

STEAMED MUD CRAB WITH SPICY TAMARIND SAUCE

SERVES 4

2 small mud crabs, about 1.25 kg (2 lb 12 oz) in total

2 stems lemongrass, outer leaves discarded, bruised

4 spring onions (scallions), trimmed

3 cm (1 inch) piece fresh ginger, sliced lengthways

SPICY TAMARIND SAUCE

2 tablespoons vegetable oil

3 garlic cloves, crushed

½ teaspoon white peppercorns, crushed

3 tablespoons fish sauce

2 teaspoons sambal oelek

1 tablespoon tamarind paste

3 tablespoons Chinese rice wine

1 **Kill the mud crabs humanely** by putting them in the freezer for 2 hours. Using a heavy cleaver, chop each into four pieces. Remove the soft internal organs and the roe, and rinse the cavities clean.

2 **Line a bamboo steamer** with baking paper and punch with holes. Arrange the lemongrass, spring onion and ginger slices on top in a single layer. Top with a single layer of the crab sections (the steaming may have to be done in batches). Sit the steamer over a wok of simmering water and steam, covered, for 12–15 minutes per batch, or until the flesh is cooked and the shells are bright red.

3 **To make the sauce,** heat the oil in a small saucepan over medium heat and add the garlic and peppercorns. When the garlic starts to brown, add the fish sauce, sambal oelek, tamarind, rice wine and 3 tablespoons of water. Simmer for 2 minutes, then remove and keep warm until ready to serve.

4 **To serve,** pile the crab on a serving platter and pour the sauce over the top.

Note: Steamed rice is the traditional accompaniment, but crusty bread is perfect for soaking up the sauce.

ROLLED FISH FILLETS WITH LEMON DILL CREAM

SERVES 4

1 lemon

8 x 70 g (2½ oz) skinless sole or flathead fillets, bones removed

8 dill sprigs

LEMON DILL CREAM

125 ml (4 fl oz/½ cup) white wine

125 ml (4 fl oz/½ cup) fish or chicken stock

½ small onion, finely chopped

250 ml (9 fl oz/1 cup) thick (double/ heavy) cream

½ teaspoon finely grated lemon zest

3 tablespoons lemon juice

30 g (1 oz) unsalted butter, chopped

2 tablespoons chopped dill

1   **Preheat a kettle** or covered barbecue to medium indirect heat.

2   **Peel the rind** and the white pith from the lemon. Using a small sharp knife, cut between the lemon membranes to release the fruit segments.

3   **Coil each fish fillet** around 1 or 2 lemon segments and a sprig of dill, leaving the dill poking up through the top. Secure with a toothpick and season with salt and freshly ground black pepper. Transfer to a lightly oiled disposable foil tray and place on the barbecue. Lower the lid and cook for 20 minutes, or until the fish flakes when tested with a fork.

4   **While the fish is cooking,** make the lemon dill cream. Put the wine, stock and onion in a small saucepan and simmer for 10–15 minutes, or until reduced to 80 ml (2½ fl oz/⅓ cup). Stir in the cream, lemon zest and lemon juice and simmer for a further 2–3 minutes, or until thickened slightly. Remove from the heat, strain to remove the onion, then stir in the butter and dill. Add salt and freshly ground black pepper to taste.

5   **Arrange 2 fish coils** on each serving plate. Remove the skewers and drizzle with the lemon dill cream. Serve with steamed green beans and baby potatoes.

SPICY WHOLE SNAPPER WITH A WINE BUTTER SAUCE

1 kg (2 lb 4 oz) whole snapper, cleaned and scaled

2 celery stalks, sliced on the diagonal

2 red capsicums (peppers), sliced on the diagonal

3 spring onions (scallions), thinly sliced

125 ml (4 fl oz/½ cup) white wine

1 tablespoon shichimi togarashi or nanami togarashi seasoning (see Note)

1 lemon, halved lengthways and thinly sliced

40 g (1½ oz) unsalted butter, chopped

1 Preheat a kettle or covered barbecue to medium indirect heat.

2 Trim the snapper fins using kitchen scissors. Wash the fish well and pat dry with paper towels. Take two sheets of foil large enough to encase the fish and lay them on a flat surface. Top with the same amount of baking paper. Fold edges into a tight, secure seam to form a large waterproof casing for the fish.

3 Spread the celery, capsicum and spring onion in the centre of the baking paper, then lay the fish lengthways over the vegetables. Pour the wine over and around the fish and sprinkle generously with salt, freshly ground black pepper and the Japanese seasoning. Overlap the lemon slices along the centre of the fish, then dot with butter and enclose the paper over the fish. Fold the ends in several times to seal in the liquid.

4 Put the fish parcel on the barbecue grill, then lower the lid and cook for about 15 minutes, or until the fish flakes when tested in the thickest part with a fork. Serve hot, with rice and lightly steamed green vegetables.

Note: Shichimi togarashi is also known as Japanese seven-spice and is often sprinkled over Japanese noodle dishes, soups and one-pots. This peppery, spicy seasoning generally contains a mixture of dried red chilli flakes, black pepper, sesame seeds, poppy seeds, hemp seeds, seaweed flakes and dried mandarin or orange peel. Nanami togarashi is a similar seasoning. They are both available from Japanese and speciality food stores.

MARINATED BLUE EYE WRAPPED IN BANANA LEAVES

SERVES 6

MARINADE

2 teaspoons ground turmeric

2 tablespoons olive oil

1 garlic clove, crushed

finely grated zest of 1 lemon

2 tablespoons lemon juice

¼ teaspoon cayenne pepper

6 x 200 g (7 oz) blue eye fillets or other
  firm thick white fish fillets

banana leaves, cut into twelve 15 cm
  (6 inch) squares

green salad and lemon wedges, to serve

1 Mix all the marinade ingredients together in a non-metallic dish. Season with salt and ground pepper. Place the fish fillets into the dish, and cover and refrigerate for 1 hour, turning occasionally.

2 Remove the fish fillets from the marinade and pat dry with paper towel. Place each fillet onto a square of banana leaf. Top with another leaf and secure with toothpicks.

3 Cook the wrapped fish on a barbecue grill plate or chargrill pan over medium heat for 8–10 minutes, turning once, or until the fish is cooked — this may depend on thickness of fish fillets.

4 Serve with tossed green salad leaves and lemon wedges.

SOUTHERN INDIAN SEAFOOD CURRY

SERVES 4

2 tablespoons vegetable oil

½ teaspoon fenugreek seeds

10 fresh curry leaves

2 green chillies, split lengthways

1 red onion, sliced

1 tablespoon tamarind concentrate

½ teaspoon ground turmeric

½ teaspoon paprika

½ teaspoon salt

½ teaspoon ground black pepper

375 ml (13 fl oz/1½ cups) coconut milk

750 g (1 lb 10 oz) mixed seafood, such as snapper or firm white fish fillets, cut into pieces; prawns (shrimp), peeled and deveined, tails intact; scallops; squid, sliced into rings

400 g (14 oz) tinned chopped tomatoes

1 **Heat the oil** in a saucepan, add the fenugreek seeds and cook over medium heat until they pop. Add the curry leaves, chillies and onion and cook for 8 minutes, or until the onion is soft.

2 **Add the tamarind,** turmeric, paprika, salt, pepper, and half the coconut milk. Bring to the boil, reduce the heat to a simmer and add the seafood. Cook for 8 minutes, or until it changes colour, turning the seafood during cooking.

3 **Add the tomatoes** and the remaining coconut milk. Cover and cook for a further 4 minutes, or until the seafood is tender.

BAKED FISH WITH MACE-INFUSED COCONUT MILK

SERVES 4

2 x 700 g (1 lb 9 oz) whole snappers, cleaned

1 teaspoon freshly cracked black pepper

½ teaspoon mild paprika

½ teaspoon ground turmeric

270 ml (9½ fl oz) coconut milk

2 pieces dried mace blade

½ large green chilli, split lengthways

¼ teaspoon salt

3–4 teaspoons lemon juice

100 g (3½ oz) snow peas (mangetout), trimmed and shredded lengthways

1 small red capsicum (pepper), shredded lengthways into strips

1 small yellow capsicum (pepper), shredded lengthways into strips

1 handful basil

1 handful coriander (cilantro) leaves

1 Preheat the oven to 200°C (400°F/Gas 6). Trim the tail and fins, and score the fish on the thickest part of the flesh with 2–3 insertions on the diagonal to ensure the fish is cooked evenly.

2 Put the fish on a large roasting tray lined with non-stick baking paper. Bake for 20 minutes, or until the flesh comes away from the bone when tested with the tip of a knife.

3 In a saucepan, add the pepper, paprika and turmeric and cook over high heat for 1–2 minutes, shaking the saucepan, or until aromatic. Reduce the heat to medium, and add the coconut milk, mace, chilli, and salt. Cook for 4 minutes, or until the oil comes to the surface. Add the lemon juice to taste. Set aside, covered with a lid to keep warm.

4 In a small bowl, combine the snow peas, capsicum, basil and coriander leaves, and toss lightly.

5 To serve, carefully place the fish on a serving platter. Discard the mace from the sauce, spoon over the fish, and arrange the salad scattered on top of the fish.

BAKED FISH FILLETS WITH TOMATO, FENNEL AND OLIVES

SERVES 4

1 tablespoon olive oil

1 red onion, finely diced

3 teaspoons Hungarian sweet paprika

1 bay leaf

100 ml (3½ fl oz) dry white wine

300 ml (10½ fl oz) fish stock

400 g (14 oz) tinned chopped tomatoes

2 baby fennel bulbs, finely sliced

4 x 180 g (6½ oz) pieces perch fillets, skinned, or other firm white fillets

finely grated zest of 1 lemon

1 small baguette, cut into 8 slices

50 g (1¾ oz/½ cup) grated parmesan cheese

60 g (2¼ oz/⅓ cup) Spanish black olives

1 small handful parsley

1 **Preheat the oven** to 180°C (350°F/Gas 4).

2 **Heat the oil** in a frying pan over medium heat. Add the onion and cook, stirring occasionally, for 6 minutes, or until softened and lightly golden. Add the paprika and bay leaf and cook for 2 minutes, or until fragrant. Stir in the wine and cook for 1 minute. Add the stock and tomatoes, stir and bring to the boil. Reduce the heat and simmer for 15 minutes.

3 **In a 35 cm x 28 cm** (14 x 11¼ inch) ceramic baking dish, arrange the fennel to cover the base, then place the fish evenly down the centre of the dish. Pour the tomato sauce over the fish, and sprinkle with half the lemon zest. Bake for 20 minutes, or until the fish is cooked and the fennel is tender.

4 **Lightly toast the bread slices** under the grill (broiler), then remove and top evenly with the cheese and grill until the cheese is melted and golden brown.

5 **To serve**, carefully remove the fish and fennel onto a serving plate, spoon the sauce over the fish and top with the olives, remaining lemon zest and parsley. Serve with the cheese bread.

SUMAC-CRUSTED TUNA WITH SAFFRON RICE

SERVES 4

2 tablespoons olive oil

1 tablespoon sumac (lemon-flavoured spice)

1 garlic clove, crushed

4 x 200 g (7 oz) tuna steaks

SAFFRON RICE

300 g (10½ oz/1½ cups) jasmine rice

pinch saffron threads

1 garlic clove, crushed

3 tablespoons chopped coriander (cilantro) leaves, plus extra whole leaves, to garnish (optional)

1 **Combine the oil,** sumac and garlic and brush over the tuna. Season well with salt and pepper. Heat an oiled barbecue grill plate or chargrill pan over medium heat and cook the tuna for 4 minutes on each side, or until cooked as desired.

2 **Meanwhile,** combine the rice, 750 ml (26 fl oz/1½ cups) of water, saffron and garlic in a saucepan and bring to the boil over high heat. Reduce the heat to low, cover, and simmer for 15 minutes, stirring occasionally, until the rice is tender. Fluff with a fork. Stir in the chopped coriander.

3 **Serve the tuna** on the saffron rice, garnished with coriander.

RAINBOW TROUT WITH SALMON ROE BUTTER

SERVES 4

4 rainbow trout, cleaned and scaled

1 large lime or lemon, finely sliced

12 lemon thyme sprigs

olive oil, for brushing

SALMON ROE BUTTER

50 g (1¾ oz) butter, softened

1 teaspoon lime or lemon juice

½ teaspoon chopped tarragon

½ teaspoon snipped chives

1 tablespoon salmon roe (see Note)

1 **Preheat a barbecue flat plate** to medium. Rinse each trout in cold water and pat dry inside and out with paper towels. Fill each trout cavity with slices of lime or lemon, put 3 sprigs of lemon thyme in each and season with salt and freshly ground pepper.

2 **Lightly brush the hotplate** and the trout with oil. Barbecue the trout for about 4 minutes, then turn and grill for a further 4 minutes, or until cooked through.

3 **While the trout** are cooking, make the salmon roe butter. In a bowl, beat the butter until smooth and stir in the lime or lemon juice, tarragon and chives. Gently fold in the salmon roe and season with freshly ground pepper.

4 **Arrange the trout** on four serving plates. Put a generous dollop of the salmon roe butter on each trout and serve immediately.

Note: Salmon roe is available at most seafood stores and is sold either in small jars or by weight.

MOROCCAN STUFFED SARDINES

SERVES 4

COUSCOUS STUFFING
75 g (2½ oz) couscous

2 tablespoons olive oil

2 tablespoons finely chopped
dried apricots

3 tablespoons raisins

1 tablespoon flaked toasted almonds

1 tablespoon chopped parsley

1 tablespoon chopped mint

grated zest of 1 orange

2 tablespoons orange juice

1 teaspoon finely chopped preserved
lemon rind (optional)

1 teaspoon ground cinnamon

½ teaspoon harissa

16 large fresh or preserved vine leaves

16 large fresh sardines, butterflied

oil, for brushing

lemon wedges, to serve

400 g (14 oz) thick plain yoghurt

1 **Start by making** the couscous stuffing. Put the couscous in a bowl and add half the oil and 50 ml (1¾ fl oz) of boiling water. Stir and leave for 10 minutes to allow the couscous to absorb the liquid. Fluff up the couscous grains with a fork and add the remaining oil and stuffing ingredients. Season to taste and mix well.

2 **Preheat a barbecue flat plate** to medium. If you are using fresh vine leaves, bring a saucepan of water to the boil and blanch the leaves in batches for 30 seconds, then remove and pat dry on paper towels. If you are using preserved vine leaves, simply rinse and pat them dry.

3 **Divide the couscous** stuffing between the sardines, saving any leftover couscous for serving time. Fold the sardine fillets back together to enclose the stuffing. Gently wrap a vine leaf around each sardine and secure with a toothpick.

4 **Lightly brush the hotplate** with oil and cook the sardines for 6 minutes, turning halfway through cooking. Serve hot with lemon wedges, a dollop of yoghurt and any remaining couscous.

STIR-FRIED PRAWNS AND ASPARAGUS

SERVES 4

1 kg (2 lb 4 oz) raw prawns (shrimp)

2 tablespoons peanut oil

3 tablespoons lime juice

2 teaspoons ground coriander

200 g (7 oz) snow peas (mangetout), trimmed

175 g (6 oz/1 bunch) asparagus, cut into 3 cm (1¼ inch) lengths

4 spring onions (scallions), cut into 3 cm (1¼ inch) lengths

5 cm (2 inch) piece of ginger, peeled and julienned

2 teaspoons cornflour (cornstarch)

125 ml (4 fl oz/½ cup) chicken stock

2 tablespoons coriander (cilantro) leaves

steamed rice, to serve

1 **Peel and devein the prawns,** leaving the tails intact.

2 **Whisk together** 1 tablespoon of peanut oil, the lime juice and ground coriander. Put the prawns into a non-metallic bowl, pour over the marinade, cover with plastic wrap and refrigerate for 20 minutes.

3 **Heat the wok** over high heat, add the remaining oil and swirl to coat. Drain the prawns, reserving the marinade. Toss the prawns in the wok for 2–3 minutes, or until pink. Remove the prawns from the wok and set aside.

4 **Toss the snow peas,** asparagus, spring onions and ginger in the wok for 2 minutes. Reduce heat to medium. Blend the cornflour with 1 tablespoon of water to form a smooth paste. Add to the wok with the remaining marinade, chicken stock and cornflour mixture. Bring to the boil and boil for 1 minute. Toss in the prawns, and sprinkle with the coriander leaves. Serve with steamed rice.

Note: It is important that the marinade boils in order to kill any bacteria present.

BARBECUE FISH WITH GREEN BEAN SALAD

SERVES 4

MARINADE

3 tablespoons grapeseed oil

2 teaspoons grated lemon zest

2 tablespoons lemon juice

2 teaspoons baharat (Middle Eastern spice mix from supermarkets)

GREEN BEAN SALAD

225 g (8 oz) green beans, trimmed

1 zucchini (courgette)

1 small carrot, peeled

½ red onion, finely sliced into wedges

salad dressing

2 tablespoons grapeseed oil

1 tablespoon lemon juice

1 teaspoon honey

½ teaspoon baharat

4 firm white fish fillets (800 g/1 lb 12 oz), such as snapper

olive oil

100 g (3½ oz) mixed salad leaves or baby rocket (arugula) leaves

lemon wedges, to serve

1 **To make the marinade,** combine the oil, lemon zest and juice and the baharat in a non-metallic dish. Coat the fish in the marinade and set aside for 30 minutes.

2 **To make the salad,** shred or finely slice the beans. Using a vegetable peeler, cut the zucchini and carrot into fine strips. Put all the ingredients into a large bowl. Combine the salad dressing ingredients and just prior to serving, pour over the salad and toss well.

3 **Preheat a barbecue flat plate** or grill plate. Lightly coat with the oil. Cook the fillets for 1 minute on each side to seal, then lower the heat and cook for 2–3 minutes on each side, or until just cooked through. The cooking time will depend on the thickness of the fillets. Brush with the marinade one or two times.

4 **To serve,** divide the salad leaves or rocket onto serving plates, pile the bean salad over and top each with a fish fillet. Serve with lemon wedges.

LINGUINE WITH FLAKED SALMON AND ASPARAGUS

SERVES 4

2 x 200 g (7 oz) salmon fillets

2 teaspoons finely grated lemon zest

1 tablespoon olive oil

350 g (12 oz/2 bunches) asparagus, trimmed

300 g (10½ oz) linguine

2 tablespoons pine nuts, toasted

6 bulb spring onions (scallions), finely chopped, including half of the green stem

150 g (5½ oz/1 bunch) rocket (arugula), stems removed,

leaves chopped in half

HERB SALSA

2 garlic cloves, peeled

2 anchovy fillets

4 tablespoons extra virgin olive oil

2 tablespoons lemon juice

1 tablespoon finely chopped basil

2 tablespoons finely chopped parsley

1 tablespoon baby capers, rinsed and squeezed dry

1 Put the salmon fillets in a large bowl. Add the lemon zest, oil and salt and pepper and massage well into the fillets. Arrange two large squares of baking paper on a clean surface and wrap up each fish fillet to make a secure parcel. Make sure you fold in the sides as you go so that no juice will escape during the steaming process. Place the wrapped fillets in a steamer and cover with a lid. Sit the steamer over a saucepan or wok of boiling water and steam for 10 minutes, or until the fish is just cooked all the way through. Remove the fish from the baking paper and pour off any juices, then set aside to cool.

2 Meanwhile, cut the asparagus spears into 4 cm (1½ inch) lengths on the diagonal. Place the asparagus in the steamer and steam for about 3 minutes.

3 To make the herb salsa, crush the garlic and anchovies with a mortar and pestle. Combine the paste in a bowl with the oil and lemon juice. Stir in the basil, parsley and capers and season with freshly ground black pepper.

4 Cook the linguine in salted boiling water for 8–10 minutes, or until al dente. Drain.

5 Combine the pine nuts, spring onion, asparagus and linguine in a large bowl, add the salsa and and toss through gently. Carefully flake in the salmon and add the rocket leaves. Lightly toss all of the ingredients together, season to taste, then serve the pasta with an extra grind of pepper.

MAHI MAHI WITH ROAST TOMATOES

SERVES 4

6 roma (plum) tomatoes

150 g (5½ oz) marinated feta cheese,
plus 4 tablespoons of the oil marinade

2 tablespoons finely chopped oregano

1 teaspoon finely grated lemon zest

sea salt, to taste

4 x 200 g (7 oz) mahi mahi or any other
firm white fish fillets, halved

250 g (9 oz) baby green beans, trimmed

400 g (14 oz) tin butterbeans (lima
beans), drained and rinsed

80 g (2¾ oz/½ cup) ligurian olives

1 handful flat-leaf (Italian) parsley

1 Preheat the oven to 200°C (400°F/Gas 6) and line a
baking tray with baking paper. Place the tomatoes, cut side
up, on the tray and drizzle with 1 tablespoon of the feta oil.
Roast in the oven for 40 minutes. When the tomatoes are
soft and starting to caramelize, remove from the oven and
set aside.

2 Put the oregano, lemon zest, 2 tablespoons of the feta
oil, sea salt and freshly ground black pepper in a small
bowl and stir to combine. Cut out four 30 cm (12 inch)
square sheets of baking paper. Place two pieces of fish side
by side in the centre of each square and spoon on some
of the oregano marinade. Carefully wrap the fillets into
secure parcels so they don't leak, then place them in a large
steamer in a single layer, seam side up, and cover with a lid.

3 Sit the steamer over a saucepan or wok of boiling water
and steam for about 10–15 minutes, or until the fish flakes
easily when tested with a fork. Using a spatula, carefully
remove the parcels from the steamer and rest on a plate.
Put the baby beans in the same steamer and cover with a
lid. Steam for 7 minutes.

4 To serve, make a free-form stack with the fish fillets,
roasted tomatoes, baby beans, butterbeans, olives,
parsley and feta. Drizzle with any extra steamer juices
plus the remaining feta oil and season with freshly ground
black pepper.

BARRAMUNDI WITH BEETROOT MASH

SERVES 4

30 bay leaves

2 beetroot (beets), peeled and chopped into

4 cm (1½ inch) pieces

3 roasting potatoes, chopped into 4 cm (1½ inch) pieces

4 tablespoons thick (double/heavy) cream

2 teaspoons aged balsamic vinegar

100 g (3½ oz) butter

1 lemon, sliced

4 barramundi or any firm white fish fillets

1 teaspoon lemon juice

3 teaspoons baby salted capers, rinsed and squeezed dry

3 teaspoons finely chopped dill

1 **Line a large steamer** with the bay leaves. Add the beetroot and cover with a lid. Sit the steamer over a saucepan or wok of boiling water and steam for 20 minutes. Add the potato and steam for a further 20 minutes, or until cooked through.

2 **Put the beetroot** and potato in a saucepan and quickly mash with the cream, vinegar and 20 g (¾ oz) of the butter. Season well, and cover to keep warm.

3 **Line a steamer** with baking paper and punch with holes. Top with the lemon slices, then place the fish fillets on top in a single layer. Cover with a lid and steam for 5 minutes, or until cooked through when tested.

4 **Meanwhile,** melt the remaining butter in a non-stick frying pan over medium–low heat and cook for 3 minutes, or until the butter starts to brown. Add the lemon juice, capers and dill and stir until combined. Serve immediately drizzled over the fish and beetroot mash. Delicious with steamed greens.

STUFFED SQUID WITH FISH AND SPINACH

SERVES 4

50 g (1¾ oz/1 cup) baby English spinach

250 g (9 oz) redfish or other firm white fish fillets, skin and bones removed

1 egg

3 tablespoons thick (double/heavy) cream

1 tablespoon tomato paste (concentrated purée)

1 tablespoon lemon juice

2 garlic cloves, roughly chopped

4 raw prawns (shrimp), peeled, deveined and roughly chopped

8 small squid tubes, about 15 cm (6 inches) long

1 tablespoon finely chopped basil

lemon wedges, to serve

SAUCE

1 tablespoon extra virgin olive oil

2 garlic cloves, crushed

200 ml (7 fl oz) dry white wine

1 bay leaf

½ teaspoon vegetable stock powder

1 large vine-ripened tomato, peeled, seeded and finely diced

1 tablespoon cream (whipping)

a dash of Tabasco sauce, or to taste

1 **Wash the spinach leaves,** add to a saucepan over low heat and stir until wilted. Squeeze all excess moisture from the spinach and place in a food processor with the fish, egg, cream, tomato paste, lemon juice and garlic. Purée for 5 minutes, or until a smooth paste is formed. Stir in the prawns and season.

2 **Using a piping bag** or a teaspoon, put the fish mixture inside the squid tubes and secure the open ends with toothpicks. Make sure the tubes are only two-thirds full as the squid will shrink as it cooks.

3 **Arrange the squid** in a single layer on a plate that will fit inside a steamer, put the plate in the steamer and cover with a lid. Sit the steamer over a saucepan or wok of boiling water and steam for 25 minutes, or until cooked.

4 **To make the sauce,** heat the oil in a saucepan over medium heat. Cook the garlic for 1 minute, or until fragrant, then add the wine, bay leaf and stock powder. Bring to the boil, then reduce the heat and simmer for 5 minutes, or until reduced by a quarter. Add the tomato and simmer for 5 minutes, then stir in the cream and Tabasco sauce. Season to taste. Divide the sauce among serving plates, place the squid on top and sprinkle with basil. Serve with lemon wedges.

STEAMED SWORDFISH WITH RISONI AND HERB PESTO

SERVES 6

400 g (14 oz/2 cups) risoni

2 tablespoons olive oil

2 teaspoons grated lemon zest

6 x 175 g (6 oz) swordfish steaks, halved horizontally

90 g (3¼ oz/2 cups) baby English spinach

1 lemon, cut into wedges

HERB PESTO

1 large handful basil

1 large handful parsley

50 g (1¾ oz/1 heaped cup) baby English spinach

50 g (1¾ oz/⅓ cup) pistachio nuts

40 g (1½ oz) parmesan cheese, chopped

2 garlic cloves, chopped

1 tablespoon finely grated lemon zest

4 tablespoons olive oil

1 **Put the risoni**, 1 tablespoon of olive oil and 1.125 litres (39 fl oz/4½ cups) of water in a saucepan and cover with a lid. Bring to the boil over high heat, then reduce the heat to very low and simmer for 12 minutes, or until the pasta is just *al dente* and there is barely any liquid in the pan. Spoon into a large bowl and keep warm.

2 **Combine the lemon zest,** remaining oil and salt and pepper in a non-metallic bowl, add the swordish and gently toss in the mixture. Cover and leave to marinate.

3 **Meanwhile,** to make the pesto, put all the ingredients except for the oil in a food processor. Pulse until roughly chopped (not too smooth), then tip into a bowl and stir in the olive oil. Season with salt and freshly ground pepper. Stir the pesto through the cooked pasta, then fold in the baby spinach — it will start to wilt in the heat of the pasta. Season to taste and keep warm.

4 **Line a steamer** with baking paper and punch with holes. Add the swordfish steaks and cover with a lid. Steam for 8–10 minutes, then remove and rest for 2 minutes.

5 **Divide the pasta** among serving plates and top each with two pieces of swordfish. Sprinkle with extra pepper and serve with a wedge of lemon.

FISH CUTLETS WITH GINGER AND CHILLI

SERVES 4

4 x 175 g (6 oz) firm white fish cutlets, such as snapper or blue-eye

5 cm (2 inch) piece of ginger, shredded

2 garlic cloves, chopped

4 red chillies, seeded and chopped

2 tablespoons chopped coriander (cilantro) stems

3 spring onions (scallions), cut into short, fine shreds

2 tablespoons lime juice

1 **Line a steamer** with banana leaves or baking paper and punch with holes. Place the fish in the steamer, top with the ginger, garlic, chilli and coriander and cover with a lid. Sit the steamer over a wok or saucepan of boiling water and steam for about 8–10 minutes, or until the fish flakes easily.

2 **Sprinkle the spring onion** and lime juice over the fish, cover and steam for an extra 30 seconds. Serve with steamed jasmine rice.

WHOLE SNAPPER WITH ASIAN FLAVOURS

SERVES 2

800 g (1 lb 12 oz) whole snapper, scaled and gutted

3 lemongrass stems

1 handful coriander (cilantro) leaves

3 cm (1¼ inch) piece of ginger, cut into thin matchsticks

1 large garlic clove, cut into thin slivers

2 tablespoons soy sauce

3 tablespoons oil

1 tablespoon fish sauce

1 small red chilli, seeded and finely chopped

1 **Score the fish** with diagonal cuts on both sides.

2 **Cut each stem of lemongrass** into three and lightly squash each piece with the end of the handle of a large knife. Put half the lemongrass in the middle of a large piece of foil and lay the fish on top. Put the remaining lemongrass and half the coriander leaves in the cavity of the fish.

3 **Mix the ginger,** garlic, soy sauce, oil, fish sauce and chilli together, then drizzle the mixture over the fish.

4 **Enclose the fish in the foil,** place it in a large steamer and cover with a lid. Sit the steamer over a wok or saucepan of boiling water and steam for 25 minutes, or until the flesh of the fish is opaque and white. Scatter with the remaining coriander leaves and serve with stir-fried Asian greens and steamed rice.

CHILLI CRAB

SERVES 4

1 kg (2 lb 4 oz) fresh blue swimmer crabs

vegetable oil, for deep-frying

3 garlic cloves, crushed

2 teaspoons grated fresh ginger

3 small red chillies, finely chopped

4 spring onions (scallions), finely chopped

125 ml (4 fl oz/½ cup) tomato sauce (ketchup)

3 tablespoons chicken stock

½ teaspoon salt

1 tablespoon sugar

2 tablespoons sweet chilli sauce

2 tablespoons hoisin sauce

1 tablespoon dark soy sauce

1 **To prepare the crab,** lift the apron (the small flap on the underside of the shell) and prise off the top hard shell. Remove any organs and the feather-like grey gills. Cut each crab into four pieces.

2 **Fill a wok** one-third full of oil and heat to 180°C (350°F), or until a cube of bread dropped in the oil browns in 15 seconds. Add the crab in batches and deep-fry for 1 minute. Drain on crumpled paper towels.

3 **Drain all but 1 tablespoon of oil** from the wok, add the garlic, ginger, chilli and spring onion and cook for 2 minutes.

4 **Combine the remaining ingredients,** add to the wok and cook for 2–3 minutes, or until reduced slightly. Add the crab and toss to coat. Reduce the heat to low, then cover and cook for 3 minutes, or until the crab is cooked through. Serve with bowls of water for rinsing hands while eating.

BUTTER PRAWN CURRY

SERVES 4

50 g (1¾ oz) ghee or butter

1 onion, cut into wedges

2 garlic cloves, crushed

2 teaspoons ground cumin

1 teaspoon mild paprika

2 teaspoons garam masala

2 teaspoons ground coriander

2 tablespoons tandoori paste

2 tablespoons tomato paste (purée)

200 g (7 oz/1 cup) crushed tomatoes

300 ml (10½ fl oz) pouring cream

250 ml (9 fl oz/1 cup) coconut cream

1 cinnamon stick

750 g (1 lb 10 oz) raw prawns (shrimp),
    peeled and deveined, tails intact

2 teaspoons sugar

1 tablespoon lemon juice

coriander (cilantro) leaves, to serve

1 Heat a wok over high heat, add the ghee and swirl to coat. Add the onion and cook for 2–3 minutes to soften, then add the garlic, cumin, paprika, garam masala and ground coriander and cook for 30 seconds.

2 Stir in the tandoori and tomato pastes and cook for 1 minute, stirring constantly. Add the crushed tomatoes, cream, coconut cream and cinnamon stick and cook for 5 minutes, or until thickened.

3 Add the prawns and cook for 2–3 minutes, or until pink and cooked through. Stir in the sugar and lemon juice. Garnish with the coriander and serve with basmati rice.

JASMINE TEA STEAMED FISH

SERVES 4

200 g (7 oz/2⅔ cups) jasmine tea leaves

100 g (3½ oz) ginger, finely sliced

4 spring onions (scallions), cut into
  5 cm (2 inch) lengths

4 x 200 g (7 oz) firm white fish fillets
  (such as snapper, barramundi or
  blue-eye)

GINGER AND SPRING ONION SAUCE

125 ml (4 fl oz/½ cup) fish stock

3 tablespoons light soy sauce

3 spring onions (scallions), finely sliced

1 tablespoon finely shredded fresh
  ginger

2 teaspoons sugar

1 large red chilli, seeded and sliced

1 **Line a double steamer** with baking paper and punch with holes. Arrange the tea, ginger and spring onion in the bottom basket and cover with a lid. Sit the steamer over a wok or saucepan of boiling water and steam for 10 minutes, or until the tea is moist and fragrant.

2 **Lay the fish fillets** in a single layer in the top basket and cover with the lid. Steam for 5–10 minutes, depending on the thickness of the fillet. To test for doneness, insert a skewer into the thickest part of the fillet — there should be no resistance. Remove from the steamer.

3 **Meanwhile,** to make the sauce, combine all the ingredients and 125 ml (4 fl oz/½ cup) of water in a small saucepan and stir over low heat for 5 minutes, or until the sugar has dissolved. Drizzle the sauce over the fish and serve with steamed rice and your favourite Asian greens.

JAPANESE-STYLE SALMON PARCELS

SERVES 4

4 x 150 g (5½ oz) salmon steaks or cutlets

2.5 cm (1 inch) piece ginger

2 celery stalks

4 spring onions (scallions)

¼ teaspoon dashi granules (see Note)

3 tablespoons mirin (see Note)

2 tablespoons tamari (see Note)

2 teaspoons sesame seeds, toasted

1 Preheat the oven to 230°C (450°F/Gas 8). Cut four squares of baking paper large enough to enclose the salmon steaks.

2 Wipe the salmon and pat dry with paper towels. Place a salmon steak in the centre of each paper square.

3 Cut the ginger into paper-thin slices. Slice the celery and spring onions into short lengths, then lengthways into fine strips. Arrange a bundle of celery and spring onion and several slices of ginger on each salmon steak.

4 Combine the dashi, mirin and tamari in a small saucepan and heat gently until the granules dissolve. Drizzle over each salmon parcel, sprinkle with sesame seeds and carefully wrap the salmon, folding in the sides to seal in all the juices.

5 Arrange the parcels on a baking tray and cook for about 12 minutes, or until tender. (The paper will puff up when the fish is cooked.) Do not overcook or the salmon will dry out. Serve immediately, as standing time can spoil the fish.

Note: Dashi, mirin and tamari are all available from Japanese food stores and most large supermarkets.

THAI GINGER FISH WITH CORIANDER BUTTER

SERVES 4

60 g (2¼ oz) butter, at room temperature

1 tablespoon finely chopped coriander (cilantro) leaves

2 tablespoons lime juice

1 tablespoon vegetable oil

1 tablespoon grated palm sugar or soft brown sugar

4 long red chillies, seeded and chopped

2 lemongrass stems, trimmed and halved

4 x 200 g (7 oz) firm white fish fillets (such as blue-eye or john dory)

1 lime, finely sliced

1 tablespoon finely shredded fresh ginger

1 **Thoroughly mix the butter** and coriander together and roll it into a log. Wrap the log in plastic wrap and chill in the refrigerator for at least 30 minutes, or until you are ready to serve.

2 **Combine the lime juice,** oil, sugar and chilli in a small non-metallic bowl and stir until the sugar has dissolved.

3 **Lay a piece of lemongrass** in the centre of a sheet of foil large enough to fully enclose one fish fillet. Place a fish fillet on top and smear the surface with the lime juice mixture. Top with some lime slices and ginger shreds, then wrap into a secure parcel. Repeat with the remaining ingredients to make four parcels.

4 **Line a large steamer** with baking paper and punch with holes. Lay the fish parcels on top in a single layer and cover with a lid. Sit the steamer over a wok or saucepan of boiling water and steam for 8–10 minutes, or until the fish flakes easily when tested with a fork.

5 **To serve,** place the parcels on individual serving plates and serve open with slices of coriander butter and some steamed rice and green vegetables.

SMOKED COD KEDGEREE

SERVES 6

350 g (12 oz) smoked cod fillets

30 g (1 oz) butter

1 tablespoon mustard oil or olive oil

1 onion, finely chopped

2 x 3 cm (¾ x 1¼ inch) piece ginger, grated

2 garlic cloves, crushed

1½ tablespoons medium curry powder

900 g (2 lb/5 cups) steamed basmati rice (see Note)

100 g (3½ oz/⅔ cup) frozen peas

2 tablespoons lemon juice

1 handful coriander (cilantro) leaves, chopped

1 handful flat-leaf (Italian) parsley, chopped

3 eggs, hard-boiled

2 tablespoons fried shallots (see Note)

1   Line a steamer with foil and punch with holes. Place the cod fillets in a single layer on top and cover with a lid. Sit the steamer over a saucepan or wok of boiling water and steam for 8–10 minutes, or until the fish is cooked through. Set aside to cool, then remove the bones and skin and flake the flesh.

2   Heat the butter and oil in a large frying pan over medium heat, add the onion, ginger and garlic and cook, stirring, for 2 minutes, or until the onion is soft. Add the curry powder and stir for 2 minutes, or until fragrant.

3   Add the rice to the pan and stir gently until the grains are separated. Stir in the peas and cook until the rice is heated through and is well coated. Add the cod, lemon juice, coriander and parsley and mix well. Season with salt and pepper. Garnish with the hard-boiled eggs and fried shallots and serve immediately.

Note: Kedgeree also makes a delicious light supper or weekend breakfast. You will need 600 g (1 lb 5 oz/3 cups) of uncooked rice to make this quantity of cooked rice. Fried shallots are deep-fried red Asian shallots and they are usually used as a garnish, to add crunch and flavour. Look for them in the Asian section of large supermarkets or in Asian grocery stores.

SEAFOOD PHAD THAI

SERVES 4

10 raw tiger prawns or 20 small prawns (shrimp), peeled and deveined

200 g (7 oz) medium-thickness dried rice noodles

1 tablespoon dried shrimp

3 tablespoons vegetable oil

2 large eggs, lightly beaten

2 garlic cloves, crushed

1 small red chilli, finely chopped

2 tablespoons grated palm sugar or soft brown sugar

3 tablespoons lemon juice

2 tablespoons fish sauce

4 tablespoons peanuts, toasted and roughly chopped

3 spring onions (scallions), sliced on the diagonal

90 g (3¼ oz/1 cup) bean sprouts, tails trimmed

3 tablespoons coriander (cilantro) leaves

lemon wedges, to serve

1 **If using tiger prawns,** chop each one into three or four pieces, depending on size. Put the rice noodles in a bowl and cover with boiling water. Put the dried shrimp in a cup and cover with boiling water. Leave both to soak for 10 minutes, then drain. Make sure you have all the other ingredients at the ready before you start cooking.

2 **Heat the oil** in a wok over high heat until smoking. Add the beaten egg and cook for 30 seconds, then stir to break into small pieces. Add the garlic, chilli and prawns and cook for 15 seconds, stirring all the time.

3 **Add the sugar,** lemon juice and fish sauce and cook for 15 seconds, stirring and tossing in the wok. Tip in the noodles, dried shrimp and 3 tablespoons of the peanuts. Toss together in the wok to heat through before adding the spring onion and bean sprouts. Cook for a further 30 seconds, then tip onto a serving plate and scatter the coriander and remaining peanuts over the top. Serve immediately with the lemon wedges.

Note: To make this dish vegetarian, omit the prawns, shrimp paste and fish sauce. Replace the prawns with 250 g (9 oz) tofu puffs, adding them to the wok at the same time as the garlic and chilli. Replace the fish sauce with 1 tablespoon of soy sauce.

CHAR KWAY TEOW WITH CRAB

SERVES 4

150 g (5½ oz) dried thin rice noodles

3 tablespoons vegetable or peanut oil

2 red Asian or French shallots, thinly sliced

1 garlic clove, finely chopped

2 small red chillies, finely chopped

180 g (6 oz/2 cups) bean sprouts, tails trimmed

175 g (6 oz) Chinese barbecue pork or other cooked pork, cut into small pieces

3 tablespoons light soy sauce

2 tablespoons oyster sauce

700 g (1 lb 9 oz) fresh or thawed frozen crab meat

2 tablespoons chopped coriander (cilantro) leaves

1 **Put the rice noodles** in a bowl and cover with boiling water. Leave to soak for about 10 minutes, then drain.

2 **Heat the oil** in a wok and swirl to coat. When hot, add the shallots, garlic and chilli. Cook over high heat, stirring, for 2–3 minutes. Add the bean sprouts and pork pieces and cook for 2 minutes. Add the soy sauce, oyster sauce, noodles, crab meat and coriander and stir for 2 minutes, or until heated through. Add salt to taste and serve immediately.

PROVENÇAL SEAFOOD STEW WITH FENNEL

SERVES 4

4 tablespoons extra virgin olive oil

1 large onion, finely chopped

1 bulb fennel, trimmed and finely chopped

2 garlic cloves, chopped

2 sprigs thyme

pinch chilli flakes

grated zest of ½ orange

3 tablespoons Pernod

400 g (14 oz) tinned tomatoes

300 ml (10½ fl oz) fish stock

½ teaspoon saffron threads

250 g (9 oz) ling fillet

250 g (9 oz) swordfish steak

12 large raw prawns (shrimp)

25 g (1 oz/¼ cup) pitted black olives, chopped

2 tablespoons chopped parsley

cooked tagliatelle, to serve

1 **Heat the oil** in a sauté pan and fry the onion, fennel, garlic, thyme, chilli flakes and orange zest for 5 minutes, or until softened and lightly golden. Add the Pernod, bring to the boil and cook for 2–3 minutes, or until reduced by half.

2 **Stir in the tomatoes,** stock and saffron. Bring to the boil, cover and simmer for 30 minutes, or until the sauce is thickened slightly.

3 **Meanwhile,** prepare the seafood. Cut the ling and swordfish into large chunks. Peel the prawns and using a small knife, cut down the back of each one, pull out and discard the black intestinal tract and wash well. Pat the prawns dry on paper towel.

4 **Add the seafood** to the stew with the olives and parsley, return to the boil and cook for 5–10 minutes, or until the seafood is tender. Season with salt to taste. Rest for 5 minutes and serve the stew with the cooked tagliatelle, tossed with a little olive oil, if desired.

MUSSELS IN GALANGAL AND LIME LEAF BROTH

SERVES 4

6 cm (2½ inch) piece fresh galangal, peeled and sliced

1 stem lemongrass, white part only, finely sliced

1 kg (2 lb 4 oz) mussels, cleaned, beards removed

270 ml (9½ fl oz) coconut milk

1½–2 tablespoons green curry paste

4 kaffir lime leaves, finely shredded

1–1½ teaspoons sugar, plus extra to taste

3–4 teaspoons fish sauce

1 handful coriander (cilantro) leaves

1 handful mint

1 **Fill a large frying pan** with 500 ml (17 fl oz/2 cups) of water and bring to the boil. Add the galangal and the lemongrass to the frying pan and cook for 2 minutes. Add the mussels, cover tightly and cook for 3 minutes, shaking the pan. Discard any mussels that do not open. Reserve 250 ml (9 fl oz/1 cup) of the stock, the galangal and the lemongrass.

2 **In a wok,** add the coconut milk and bring to the boil. Add the curry paste, lime leaves and sugar. Stir and simmer for 3 minutes, or until the oil comes to the surface. Add the reserved galangal and lemongrass and simmer for a further 2 minutes.

3 **Return the mussels** to the wok and stir until the mussels are covered with the sauce. Add the fish sauce and extra sugar, to taste, and reserved stock to adjust flavours and mix well.

4 **In a small bowl,** combine the coriander and mint leaves. To serve, divide the mussels among four bowls and top with the fresh herbs.

CHILLI TOMATO PIZZAS WITH PRAWNS AND SCALLOPS

MAKES 8

PIZZA BASE

1½ teaspoons dried yeast

500 g (1 lb 2 oz/4 cups) strong flour

1 teaspoon sea salt flakes

1 tablespoon olive oil, plus extra
for greasing

TOMATO CHILLI SAUCE

800 g (1 lb 12 oz) tinned chopped
tomatoes

1 onion, sliced

2 garlic cloves, finely chopped

3 tablespoons olive oil

3 teaspoons oregano, chopped

1 small red chilli, finely sliced

24 raw king prawns (shrimp), peeled
and deveined, tails intact

24 scallops

oil, for brushing

zest of 2 lemons

1 teaspoon ground mace

100 g (3½ oz) rocket (arugula) leaves

1 Preheat the oven to 210°C (415°F/Gas 6–7).

2 Put the yeast, flour and salt into the bowl of an electric mixer with a dough hook, and mix well. Add 250 ml (9 fl oz/1 cup) of warm water and the oil, and mix on low speed for 5 minutes, or until soft and elastic. Alternatively, knead by hand for 10 minutes. Put the dough into a large lightly oiled bowl and cover. Stand in a warm place for 1 hour, or until doubled in size.

3 Meanwhile, put the tomatoes, onion, garlic, oil, oregano and chilli into a saucepan. Bring to the boil over high heat. Reduce the heat to low and simmer, uncovered, for 15 minutes, or until the mixture is thick. Season well with salt and pepper.

4 Lightly knead the dough on a floured surface until smooth. Cut into eight even pieces. Roll each piece into 18 cm (7 inch) diameter rounds. Place onto two large oiled baking trays. Rest for a further 10 minutes.

5 Spoon the sauce onto the bases. Arrange the prawns and scallops on top, and brush with oil. Sprinkle with the zest and mace. Bake for 15 minutes, or until golden and the seafood is opaque and cooked. Serve topped with the rocket leaves.

JANSSON'S TEMPTATION

SERVES 4

15 anchovy fillets

80 ml (3 fl oz/⅓ cup) milk

60 g (2 oz) butter

2 large onions, thinly sliced

5 potatoes, peeled, cut into

5 mm (¼ mm) slices, then julienned (cut into matchsticks)

500 g (16 fl oz/2 cups) thick (double/heavy) cream

1 **Preheat the oven** to 200°C (400°F/Gas 6). Soak the anchovies in the milk for 5 minutes to lessen their saltiness. Drain and rinse.

2 **Melt half the butter** in a frying pan and cook the onion over medium heat for 5 minutes, or until golden and tender. Chop the remaining butter into small cubes and set aside.

3 **Spread half the potato** over the base of a shallow ovenproof dish, top with the anchovies and onion and finish with the remaining potato.

4 **Pour half the cream** over the potato and scatter the butter cubes on top. Bake for 20 minutes, or until golden.

5 **Pour the remaining cream** over the top and cook for another 40 minutes, or until the potato feels tender when the point of a knife is inserted. Season with salt and pepper before serving.

SINGAPORE BLACK PEPPER CRAB

SERVES 4–6

3 tablespoons kecap manis

3 tablespoons oyster sauce

3 teaspoons caster (superfine) sugar

2 kg (4 lb 8 oz) raw blue swimmer crabs

1½ tablespoons peanut oil

40 g (1½ oz) butter

1½ tablespoons finely chopped fresh
    ginger

6 large garlic cloves, finely chopped

1–2 small red chillies, deseeded and
    finely chopped

1½ tablespoons freshly cracked black
    pepper

1½ teaspoons ground white pepper

¼ teaspoon ground coriander

2 spring onions (scallions), finely sliced

1 handful coriander (cilantro) leaves,
    roughly chopped

1 **Place the kecap manis,** oyster sauce and sugar in a small bowl. Add 3 tablespoons of water. Stir to combine, then set aside.

2 **Pull back the apron** on each crab and remove the top shell. Discard the intestines and pull off the grey feathery gills. Cut each crab into four pieces. Crack the legs with crab crackers or a meat mallet to allow the flavours to permeate the meat.

3 **Heat the peanut oil** in a large wok over high heat. Stir-fry the crab pieces in batches for about 5 minutes, or until the shell is bright orange and flesh is almost cooked, then remove from the wok.

4 **Add the butter,** ginger, garlic, chilli, black and white pepper and ground coriander to the wok and stir-fry for 30 seconds, or until fragrant. Add the sauce mixture and stir to combine. Bring to the boil and cook for 2 minutes, or until glossy.

5 **Return the crab** to the wok and toss to coat in the sauce. Cook for 2–3 minutes further to finish cooking the crab meat then garnish with the spring onion and coriander leaves and serve immediately.

Note: 1.5 kg (3 lb 5 oz) prawns (shrimp) in the shell can be substituted for the crab.

PRAWN AND WASABI MAYONNAISE ROLLS

MAKES 6

600 g (1 lb 5 oz) cooked prawns (shrimp), peeled and deveined

4 tablespoons whole-egg mayonnaise

3 teaspoons lemon juice

1¼ teaspoons wasabi paste

2 teaspoons finely chopped mint, plus extra whole leaves for topping

6 mini bread rolls

butter, for spreading (optional)

1 Lebanese (short) cucumber, finely sliced

1   Roughly chop the prawns, then combine with the mayonnaise, lemon juice, wasabi and mint. Season to taste.

2   Cut through the bread rolls, leaving them hinged. Pull a little bread out from the inside of the top half of the roll to form a slight hollow.

3   Spread each roll with a little butter, if desired, then lay a few slices of cucumber over the bottom half of each roll. Top with a couple of mint leaves, then fill the rolls with the prawn mixture and serve.

SEAFOOD BASICS

Seafood makes up the world's most numerous and diverse group of 'wild' food stocks, and can be found in all the waters of the world. This comprehensive guide to cooking with seafood includes information on the different types available and on purchasing, storing and cooking seafood. It will help you to prepare successful and delicious dishes every time.

Buying and storing seafood

BALMAIN BUGS AND OTHER CRUSTACEANS: Bugs should have no discolouration or 'blackness', particularly at the joints. Bodies and claws should be fully intact. Bodies should be free of water or liquid and should be heavy in relation to their size.

When buying live bugs, they should be active and moving freely. Nippers and claws should be intact, not broken or loose. Store live bugs covered in a damp cloth in the salad compartment of the fridge for 1–2 days. To freeze, wrap the bugs in foil, place in an airtight freezer bag and freeze for up to 3 months.

CRABS: Always buy live crabs from a reputable source as they are highly perishable. Look for lively crabs that feel heavy for their size. Crabs with worn barnacles and feet will not have just moulted — these crabs will have more meat. Mud crabs should be tied up until after they have been killed. Never buy a dead uncooked crab. Store live crabs covered in a damp cloth in a closed container in the coldest part of the fridge for 1–2 days. To freeze, wrap crabs in foil, put in an airtight bag and freeze for up to 3 months.

Cooked crabs are also highly perishable, so buy with care. Make sure they smell fresh and are undamaged and their legs and feet are drawn into the body (if they were dead when cooked, their legs will be looser). Crab meat is also available frozen, tinned and in vacuum-sealed plastic bags.

CRAYFISH: Live crayfish should feel heavy and still be fairly lively. If they have not been purged (had their guts cleaned out) before sale, crayfish need to have their guts removed before eating. Cooked crayfish should have their tails curled tightly against their bodies and smell sweet and look fresh. Never buy dead uncooked crayfish.

Store live crayfish covered in a damp cloth in the salad compartment of the fridge for 1–2 days. To freeze, wrap the crayfish in foil, place in an airtight freezer bag and freeze for up to 3 months.

FISH FILLETS/CUTLETS: Fillets or cutlets should look moist and have no signs of discolouration. The fish on display should not be sitting in liquid. Fresh fish fillets should not look dried at the edges.

Fish fillets and cutlets can be stored for 1–2 days in a covered container in the coldest part of the fridge. Alternatively, they can be frozen in airtight bags for up to 3 months.

LOBSTER: When buying a live lobster, make sure it is lively and has its tail tucked under its body. The shell should be hard — a soft shell indicates it has just moulted and is not in peak condition. The shell should have no holes and the lobster should have all its limbs. When picking up a lobster, first make sure its claws are taped together, then pick it up just behind the head using your finger and thumb. Don't grasp it around its middle as it might close up on you suddenly.

Store live lobsters covered in a damp cloth in the salad compartment of the fridge for 1–2 days. To freeze, wrap the lobster in foil, place in an airtight freezer bag and freeze for up to 3 months.

Don't buy dead uncooked lobster as there is no way of telling what condition it is in and the meat deteriorates quickly. Lobster can also be bought already cooked—it should smell sweet and look fresh.

MUSSELS: Always buy mussels from a reputable source. Mussels are farmed extensively and these are safer to eat than wild ones as mussels are filter-feeders and many harbour toxins. Fresh mussels must be bought alive, as any that are dead may be toxic. The shells should be uncracked and closed, or should close when tapped on the bench.

Store live mussels covered in a damp cloth in the salad compartment of the fridge for 1–2 days.

Fresh crabs.

Squid.

Tiger prawns.

Clams.

OCTOPUS AND SQUID: The flesh should be firm and resilient and spring back when touched. The head, tentacles and body should be intact and not loose.

Fresh octopus and squid will last for 1 to 2 days in the fridge and for about 3 months in the freezer.

OYSTERS: Ideally, an oyster should be bought live, with the shell closed. In this state, it should be heavy and full of water. If buying an open oyster, prick the cilla (little hairs around the edge of the flesh): it should retract if the oyster is alive. Look for plump, glossy oysters that smell fresh. Unopened, oysters can be kept in the fridge for up to a week. If opened, store in their liquid and eat within 24 hours. Do not freeze.

PRAWNS (SHRIMP): When buying raw prawns, avoid limp and soft ones that smell of ammonia or have any black spots or juices around the shell and head. Choose fully intact, firm and crisp prawns, with bright shells and a fresh sea scent. Most fishmongers also sell ready-cooked prawns, which takes all the bother out of the preparation.

Raw prawns will keep for 1–2 days in a covered container in the coldest part of the fridge. To freeze, place in a plastic container and cover with water — this forms a large ice block which insulates the prawns and prevents freezer burn. Freeze this way for up to 3 months. When required, thaw in the refrigerator overnight.

SCALLOPS: Scallop flesh should be pale beige to light pink, moist and glossy with a fresh sea smell. The orange or pinky red roe is also edible. Scallops are sold either still enclosed in their shells or removed from the shell (shucked). Because they deteriorate rapidly once out of the water, they are usually sold shucked and should be refrigerated quickly and used within 1 day. They can also be bought frozen.

WHOLE FISH: Fish should be considered seasonal to really get the most out of them, as supplies will vary according to spawning seasons and to fishing patterns. It is wise to buy the best fish that day, whatever it is, rather than an inferior fish just to fit a particular recipe.

Choose fish that have clear, bright and bulging eyes and avoid fish that have dull, sunken and cloudy eyes. The skin and flesh should have a lustrous appearance and feel firm. If a fish can easily be bent so its mouth can kiss its tail, it is probably past its prime. Fish with scales should have a good even coverage and if patchy-looking are best avoided. Gills should be bright (from bright to dark red, depending on species). Some fish, such as salmon and trout, are covered in a clear slime (old slime is opaque). Oily fish deteriorate faster than white fish, so be particularly vigilant when buying them.

Whole fish are best stored after they have been scaled and gutted. Store in a covered container in the coldest part of the fridge for 2–3 days.

Preparing seafood

CLEANING MUSSELS: Only use closed mussels or mussels that close when tapped on the bench. Scrub the mussels with a stiff brush and pull out the hairy beards. Discard any broken mussels, or open ones that don't close when tapped on the bench. Rinse well under cold running water.

CLEANING SQUID: To clean squid, gently pull the tentacles away from the tube—the intestines should come away at the same time. Remove the intestines from the tentacles by cutting under the eyes, then remove the beak by using your fingers to push up the centre. Pull away the soft bone. Rub the tubes under cold running water and the skin should come away easily. Wash the tubes and tentacles and drain well. The flaps can also be used. Use the body, flap and tentacles whole, or cut the body into wings.

PREPARING CRABS: If the crabs are live, freeze them for 1 hour to immobilize them. Plunge them into boiling water for 2 minutes, then drain. Wash well with a stiff brush, then pat dry. Pull the apron back from underneath the crab and separate the shells. Remove the feathery gills and intestines. Twist off the claws. Using a cleaver or large knife, cut the crabs in half. Crack the claws using crab crackers or the back of a heavy knife.

PREPARING OCTOPUS: Using a small knife, carefully cut between the head and tentacles of the octopus, just below the eyes. Grasp the body of the octopus and push the beak out and up through the centre of the tentacles with your finger. Cut the eyes from the head of the octopus by slicing a small round off, with a small sharp knife. Discard the eye section. To clean the octopus, carefully slit through one side, avoiding the ink sac, and scrape out any gut from inside. When you have slit the head open, rinse under running water to remove any remaining gut.

PREPARING SCALLOPS: If you are starting with scallops still enclosed in their shell, start by scrubbing clean the shells. For easy shucking, put it under a griller (broiler) for 1 minute to warm. Hold the scallop in a tea towel and, with a sharp knife, carefully prise open the shell. Lift off the top shell. Loosen the scallop from the shell.

With a small sharp knife, carefully slice off and discard any vein, membrane or hard white muscle from each scallop. The pinky red roe is edible but may be removed if you prefer.

SCALING AND GUTTING FISH: Fish need to be gutted fairly quickly as their digestive juices can break down and start to decompose their flesh. Preferably scale your fish outdoors, in a plastic bag or in the sink. Hold the fish firmly at the tail. Lifting it slightly, scrape against the direction of the scales with a fish scaler or sharp knife. Rinse well. Use a sharp knife to slit the belly, then remove the gut. Rinse under cold water, then pat dry with paper towel.

INDEX